THE

CHATGPT
SALES PLAYBOOK

Revolutionizing Sales with AI

LINDA BISHOP

Published by TT Books,
A Division of Thought Transformation Inc., Atlanta, Georgia.

Thought Transformation can provide training for sales professionals who want to add using AI to their sales tool kit. For more information, visit ThoughtTransformation.com.

Cover and Layout Design by Keith Bishop, Pitch Graphics.

The information in this publication is based on the opinions of the author and is not intended to render legal or professional advice of any kind on the topic. If legal advice or other expert assistance is required, the reader is advised to seek the services of a competent professional.

TTBooks
A THOUGHT TRANSFORMATION COMPANY

Table of Contents

INTRODUCTION

1. What is ChatGPT?..1

2. A Top-Level View of Tasks and Applications.............4

3. Finding New Leads Using ChatGPT..........................6

4. Getting Started on Writing Prompts.......................11

5. Researching Buyer Pain Points..............................14

6. Using AI to Write Emails to Request Meetings.........18

7. An Example of Creating a Meeting Request Email....23

8. Planning and Preparing for Meetings......................32

9. Creating Relevant Information for Sales Calls..........49

10. Stand-Out Follow-Up Strategies...........................71

11. Overcoming Barriers to a Sale.............................91

12. Self-Coaching Using ChatGPT.............................109

13. Cross-Selling to Win...132

14. AI and Social Selling on LinkedIn........................143

15. More on Writing Prompts..................................164

16. Go Time!..173

INTRODUCTION

There is a revolution taking place in the way we all work. It is driven by Artificial Intelligence (AI) and the development of systems that think and act rationally and reasonably mimic human thinking.

AI has been around for decades, but the pace of use has accelerated in the 21st Century because technology has evolved. Companies can crunch more data, and natural language processing (NLP) feeds on data.

NLP allows computers to understand text and spoken words in similar ways to humans. It enables programs like ChatGPT to assist sales pros in answering questions, composing emails and executive briefs, and speeding up the completion of many sales tasks.

Sales leaders at major corporations are exploring how AI-based technology can be used to improve outcomes. Undoubtedly, we will see many remarkable developments come to market over the next few years.

However, the best-in-class sales professionals are not waiting for their bosses or companies to tell them how to use AI to improve outcomes. They're doing what they have always done—taking charge of their careers and obtaining the necessary tools and skills to perform and win.

If you're reading this book, I would make three observations about you. First, like me, you are aware of AI and thinking about how it will impact selling. Second, you want to be a sales leader, not a lagger, and already recognize that includes developing new AI-related sales skills. And third, you are looking for a practical overview of how AI can be used to help you win.

This book contains practical skills for sales pros and descriptions of how to use ChatGPT to save time and improve outcomes.

Ultimately, this book is about closing more deals, outselling your competition, and winning in your market.

Ready to jump ahead on the learning curve? Let's go.

CHAPTER ONE

WHAT IS CHATGPT?

To understand the tool, I asked ChatGPT this question:
What is ChatGPT?

The system responded with this answer:

> *ChatGPT is an advanced language model developed by OpenAI. It is based on the GPT-3.5 architecture, which stands for "Generative Pre-trained Transformer 3.5." GPT-3.5 is trained on a massive amount of text data to understand and generate human-like responses to a wide range of prompts.*
>
> *ChatGPT is designed to engage in natural language conversations with users, providing information, answering questions, and generating coherent and contextually relevant responses. It can understand and generate text in multiple languages and has been trained on diverse topics. However, it's important to note that ChatGPT's responses are generated based on patterns and examples in its training*

> *data and do not possess true understanding or consciousness.*
>
> *OpenAI has trained ChatGPT using reinforcement learning from human feedback, combining a pre-training phase where it learns from a broad range of internet text and a fine-tuning phase where it is fine-tuned on specific datasets with human-generated responses.*
>
> *The goal of ChatGPT is to provide a useful and interactive tool that can assist users with various tasks, provide information, and engage in meaningful conversations.*

ChatGPT can answer questions and respond to prompts. **What's the difference between a question and a prompt?** Here is how the system explained the differences:

> *In the context of ChatGPT, questions and prompts serve slightly different purposes.*
>
> *A prompt in ChatGPT refers to the input given to the model to elicit a response. It can be a statement, a question, or an incomplete sentence. The prompt sets the context and provides initial information for the model to generate a relevant and coherent response. For example, a prompt could be: "Tell me about the life of Albert Einstein."*
>
> *On the other hand, a question is a specific type of prompt that seeks information or clarification. Questions typically end with a question mark and explicitly request an answer. They often begin with question words like "what," "how," "where," or "why." For example, a question prompt could be: "What are the symptoms of COVID-19?"*

> *While ChatGPT can generate responses to both prompts and questions, questions are more explicit in their intention to seek information, whereas prompts can encompass a broader range of inputs, including statements, prompts for opinions, or general conversation starters.*

When I wrote this book, ChatGPT had free and paid options. There are other tools, but I focused on this one because it is easy to use.

Once I learned more about ChatGPT, I found many ways to save time on tasks, and time is money for sales pros.

Let's take a top-level look at the type of tasks where integrating AI-generated information helps you work faster or better.

CHAPTER TWO

A TOP-LEVEL VIEW OF TASKS AND APPLICATIONS

Before we dive into tasks and applications, be aware of ChatGPT's disclaimer, which states, "ChatGPT may produce inaccurate information about people, places, or facts."

When using ChatGPT, use your critical thinking skills to assess the validity of the answers it provides. If you feel the information is vague or sketchy, discard it or verify it using trusted sources. Buyers purchase because they trust you and believe you are a competent professional and source of accurate information.

Here is a top-level view of some of the ways to apply ChatGPT to solving sales problems:

- Answering questions.
- Summarizing text.
- Personalized buyer content.
- Personalized learning.
- Content creation.

- Market, product, and topic research.
- Competitive analysis.
- Social strategies and posts to build your personal brand.
- Checking grammar and spelling.
- Writing emails.
- Generating new ideas.
- Creating presentations and videos.
- Lead generation.
- Assisting with writing.
- Presentations.
- Generating ideas.
- Answering specific questions about overcoming objections and selling situations.

Can sales pros use ChatGPT for other purposes? I'm sure the answer is "YES!"

This book isn't a comprehensive guide; it's a starting point. Let's begin with finding leads.

CHAPTER THREE

FINDING NEW LEADS USING CHATGPT

I asked, **"How can you use ChatGPT to find sales prospects in an industry?"**

Here's the response:

> To use ChatGPT to find sales prospects in an industry, you can follow these steps:
>
> - Define your target industry: Determine the specific industry or niche you want to focus on. This will help provide context for your prospecting efforts and allow ChatGPT to generate more relevant suggestions.
> - Compile a list of criteria: Identify the key criteria that define your ideal sales prospects within the industry. This may include factors such as company size, location, revenue, customer base, or any other relevant parameters.
> - Engage in a conversation with ChatGPT: Begin a conversation with ChatGPT by explaining your target

industry and the criteria you're looking for in prospects. For example, you can start by saying, "I'm looking for sales prospects in the [industry] who meet the following criteria: [criteria 1], [criteria 2], [criteria 3], etc."

- *Request prospect suggestions: Ask ChatGPT for suggestions based on your defined criteria. For instance, you can ask, "Can you provide me with a list of companies in the [industry] that meet the criteria I mentioned earlier?"*
- *Refine the conversation: Engage in a back-and-forth conversation with ChatGPT to further clarify your requirements or ask follow-up questions. You can narrow down your criteria or ask for additional details about the generated prospects.*
- *Evaluate and validate prospects: Review the generated prospect suggestions and assess their relevance to your sales goals. You can cross-reference the companies provided by ChatGPT with external sources or conduct further research to validate their suitability.*
- *Repeat and iterate: If needed, iterate the conversation with ChatGPT by refining your criteria or requesting more suggestions until you find a satisfactory list of sales prospects.*

Remember, while ChatGPT can provide you with suggestions, it's important to validate the information and conduct your own due diligence to ensure the accuracy and relevance of the generated prospects. ChatGPT can be a useful tool in the

> *prospecting process, but human judgment and verification remain crucial for successful sales efforts.*

Industries, Accounts, and Contacts

Try this experiment:

- Go to ChatGPT.
- Describe what you sell.
- Ask for industry-level recommendations for buyers that purchase what you sell.
- Pick one industry.
- Ask for recommendations for companies within that industry headquartered in your sales territory.
- Pick one company.
- Ask for the buyer's contact information, restating what you want to sell.

You will probably get answers to questions about industries and possibly companies. You will be the judge of whether they are helpful.

Asking for a buyer's name at a specific company creates a response like this:

> *I'm sorry, but as an AI language model, I don't have access to personal contact information or the specific names of individuals working at companies. It would be inappropriate and against OpenAI's use case policy to provide personal contact details without explicit consent.*
>
> *If you need to get in touch with a buyer at any specific company, I recommend visiting the official website of the company and looking for their contact information or*

> *reaching out to their customer service department for assistance.*

Global Trends, Not Company Specific

ChatGPT can help you research global trends within a specified industry but doesn't provide information about specific accounts. If you ask for news about an account, this message pops up:

> *As an AI language model with a knowledge cutoff in September 2021 and no real-time browsing capabilities, I don't have access to current news or updates. Therefore, I cannot provide you with the most recent news about <the name of the company>.*
>
> *To find the latest news about <the company>, I recommend visiting reputable news websites, searching for "<company name> news" on a search engine, or checking business news sources that regularly cover updates and developments related to the company. This will ensure you have access to the most up-to-date and accurate information about <company name>.*

So, what are the takeaways?

- If you're looking for leads, you must identify an industry, a company, and contacts.
- ChatGPT can usually provide industry-level information about the type of businesses that may purchase your products or services. The results can be helpful if you are new to selling, leading a sales

expansion effort in a new geographic location, or selling to a new category of buyers.

- ChatGPT is less successful at identifying companies within an industry. Sometimes, you get answers, but not always.
- ChatGPT cannot find contacts or contact information.

Many sales tools have been developed explicitly for lead identification. To learn about them, ask ChatGPT, "What software is available for sales professionals to find leads and the lead's contact information?"

It will give you an answer but querying a search engine offers better and broader results to this question, along with many other questions asked when hunting for leads.

Once you have a list of leads, you need to get meetings. Let's explore how ChatGPT can help accomplish that goal.

CHAPTER FOUR

GETTING STARTED ON WRITING PROMPTS

Prompts are inquiries telling ChatGPT what you want to know. The best prompts are specific and written in complete sentences. You can frame a prompt by forming a statement that starts with a phrase like, *"Tell me about . . ."* or by asking a question. Asking one question at a time improves the odds of receiving useful answers. Adding examples or scenarios to your prompts can also be helpful.

You can specify a desired format for the answer. For example, you could ask for a list, a step-by-step guide, a table, or for the answer to be formatted for a specific type of communication (e.g., email, presentation, social post).

Providing context also improves responses. The following is how ChatGPT explained what it means to provide context when asking questions:

> *Providing context in ChatGPT refers to offering additional information or background details about a specific topic or situation. Context helps the model better understand the*

scope and purpose of your question or request, enabling it to generate more accurate and relevant responses. When interacting with ChatGPT, context can be essential for achieving meaningful and contextually appropriate answers.

Here's an example to illustrate the importance of context:

Prompt without context: "Who is the president?"

This prompt lacks context, so the model might generate a response based on the most recent or widely known information available at the time of its training, which could be outdated or incorrect.

Prompt with context: "As of 2021, who is the president of the United States?"

By providing the context that the question pertains to 2021 and the United States, you're specifying the relevant time frame and location, allowing ChatGPT to generate a more accurate response based on the given context.

Similarly, when asking more complex questions or seeking assistance in specific domains, providing relevant background information, industry-specific terminology, or details about your goals can help ChatGPT understand your query more comprehensively.

For example, if you ask ChatGPT, "What are the best marketing strategies?" providing context about your target audience, industry, or budget constraints can lead to more tailored and actionable insights.

Remember that context can be provided within the prompt itself, such as including relevant details or framing your *question with specific parameters. By offering context, you help guide the model's understanding and generate more precise and helpful responses.*

ChatGPT also has a "temperature setting," which determines a response's degree of randomness. The standard temperature setting in ChatGPT is 0.7. This setting works well in most cases, but it can be adjusted to fit your needs. Higher values, like 0.8 or 0.9, make responses more random and creative, while lower values, like 0.2 or 0.3, produce more focused and deterministic responses. The setting can be changed by adding bracketed information to your query. To get specifics on how to do this, type a query into ChatGPT.

Often, you must review and refine responses by modifying prompts or asking follow-up questions before you will be satisfied with the information.

And like all selling skills, doing is the best way to learn.

CHAPTER FIVE

RESEARCHING BUYER PAIN POINTS

Sales pros know one fast route to a sale is eliminating the buyer's pain points. I asked ChatGPT, *"How do salespeople use buyer pain points within the selling cycle?"*

Here is the response:

> *Salespeople use buyer pain points within the selling cycle to understand their customers' needs, challenges, and motivations. By identifying and addressing these pain points, sales professionals can demonstrate how their products or services can provide solutions and alleviate the customers' problems. Here's how salespeople typically use buyer pain points throughout the selling cycle:*
>
> *Research and Preparation: Before engaging with potential customers, salespeople conduct research to understand their industry, market trends, and common pain points faced by customers. This information helps them tailor their approach and messaging accordingly.*

Prospecting: During the prospecting stage, salespeople identify potential leads who may be experiencing specific pain points that their offerings can address. By identifying these pain points early on, salespeople can better qualify and prioritize leads.

Needs Assessment: Once salespeople engage with prospects, they conduct a thorough needs assessment to identify their pain points in detail. This involves asking relevant questions and actively listening to understand the challenges and goals of the prospect. By empathizing with the customer's pain points, salespeople can build rapport and trust.

Value Proposition: Based on the identified pain points, salespeople tailor their value proposition to highlight how their product or service directly addresses and resolves those challenges. They articulate the unique benefits and advantages of their offerings, positioning them as solutions to the buyer's pain points.

Customized Presentations and Demonstrations: Salespeople use the buyer's pain points as a guide to customize their presentations and product demonstrations. They focus on showcasing features and functionalities that directly address the identified pain points, ensuring that the prospect sees the relevance and value of the solution.

Overcoming Objections: Salespeople anticipate objections or concerns that prospects may have and proactively address them. By acknowledging and providing solutions to the pain points that might hinder a buying decision, salespeople build credibility and trust with the prospect.

> *Closing the Sale: During the negotiation and closing stage, salespeople emphasize how their product or service effectively resolves the buyer's pain points. They reiterate the benefits, return on investment, and positive outcomes the customer can expect by making the purchase.*
>
> *Post-Sale Relationship Building: Even after the sale, salespeople continue to use the buyer's pain points as a reference point for ongoing customer support and relationship building. They ensure that the customer's pain points are continually addressed and that the product or service delivers on its promises.*
>
> *By understanding and leveraging buyer pain points throughout the selling cycle, salespeople can effectively connect with customers, build trust, and position their offerings as the ideal solutions to address the customer's challenges.*

Asking ChatGPT about a buyer's pain points is a fast and easy way to grab a collection of thoughts you can reference when working on sales tasks, from getting meetings with leads to penetrating deeper into established accounts. Even if ChatGPT doesn't offer anything that strikes you as new or surprising, validating your expertise can be helpful because it confirms you are focused on what matters to buyers.

Here are a few questions you can use as prompts to gather information and ideas:

- What are the common pain points or challenges buyers face in (your industry or market)?

- What do buyers need when choosing a vendor to purchase (product/service)?
- How do buyers prioritize needs or pain points when purchasing (product/service)?
- Are there any industry-specific pain points for buyers in the (specified industry) when buying (product/service)?

You can also list out paint points or challenges and then ask, "Which of these has the most significant impact on (profits/productivity/costs)?"

This research can be used to create emails to get meetings with leads. Let's look at how that works.

CHAPTER SIX

USING AI TO WRITE EMAILS TO REQUEST MEETINGS

I asked ChatGPT, *"When a salesperson is planning to write an email to get a meeting with a lead, what is a list of steps to take to create a strong email that convinces the buyer to agree to a meeting,"* and got this response:

> When writing an email to secure a meeting with a lead, it's important to craft a strong message that captures their attention and convinces them to agree to the meeting. Here's a list of steps you can follow to create an effective email:
>
> Research the lead: Gather information about the lead, their industry, company, and any specific pain points or challenges they may be facing. This will help you tailor your message to their needs.
>
> Write a compelling subject line: The subject line is the first thing the lead will see, so make it attention-grabbing and

concise. It should pique their curiosity or highlight a benefit they can gain from the meeting.

Personalize the email: Address the lead by their name and mention any relevant details you found during your research. Personalization helps create a connection and shows that you've put effort into understanding their specific situation.

Begin with a strong opening: Hook the reader from the start by stating a common problem or challenge they might be facing. Show empathy and understanding to engage their interest right away.

Highlight the benefits: Clearly communicate the value and benefits they can expect from meeting with you. Focus on how your product or service can solve their pain points or improve their business outcomes. Use specific examples or success stories to illustrate your points.

Keep it concise: Keep the email brief and to the point. Busy professionals often skim emails, so make sure your key message stands out. Use short paragraphs, bullet points, or subheadings to improve readability.

Call-to-action: Clearly state what you want the lead to do next. Request a specific date and time for the meeting, or offer them options to choose from. Make it easy for them to respond and provide your contact information for convenience.

Add credibility: Include any relevant industry awards, client testimonials, or case studies that showcase your expertise and track record. This helps build trust and credibility with the lead.

Professional tone and formatting: Use a professional tone throughout the email and avoid overly technical jargon. Proofread for grammar and spelling errors, and ensure the email is visually appealing and easy to read.

Follow-up plan: If you don't receive a response within a reasonable timeframe, have a plan for follow-up. Consider sending a polite reminder or exploring alternative communication channels, such as a phone call.

Remember, the key to a successful email is to make it customer-centric, addressing the lead's pain points and offering tangible benefits. Personalization, clear communication, and a compelling call-to-action are crucial elements for convincing the buyer to agree to a meeting.

Let's examine these points to see how ChatGPT can assist you in creating meeting request emails.

Research the Lead

ChatGPT can help you research top-level information about industries and the challenges and pain points experienced by buyers. If you want to research a company, you will gain more from a visit to their website. If you need to know about a buyer, check them out on LinkedIn.

Write a Compelling Subject Line

Once an email is written, you can drop the copy into ChatGPT and ask for subject line suggestions. If you get one you like, I recommend you run it through one of the many free online tools that let you score the email subject line. In general, emails with high-scoring subject lines are more likely to get opened. Use the search phrase "free tools to score email subject lines" to find options.

Personalize the Email

ChatGPT recommends, "Begin with a strong opening, highlight the benefits, keep it concise, include a call-to-action, and add credibility."

All this is good advice. The best way to put it to use is by using ChatGPT to generate a complete email. Review the email, applying your sales intelligence to determine if the email will work for your audience.

Follow-Up Plan

You must often send multiple emails to leads before they agree to meet. ChatGPT is helpful in creating a cohesive email series. Investing the time to develop a series often saves time in the long run by making it easier to fire off another email at designated intervals when buyers don't respond.

Let's work through the process of using ChatGPT to create an email to request a meeting with a lead.

Start by asking a question that generates ideas, either about industry challenges or buyer pain points.

Use the information in one of the following ways:

- Ask ChatGPT to write an email requesting a meeting with a buyer using the information.
- Select one point and ask ChatGPT to write an email requesting a meeting using only that point.

See what you get and assess:

- When mentioning a pain point, will the buyer care about eliminating it?
- Does the email clearly communicate why the meeting benefits the buyer?
- Is the email long or wordy?

At first, this may feel a little clunky, but with a little practice, you will see the benefits.

Let's look at an example.

CHAPTER SEVEN

AN EXAMPLE OF CREATING A MEETING REQUEST EMAIL

Here is an example of how ChatGPT works and what you can create in approximately 3 minutes. Since I got my start in sales in the printing industry, I created an email for a buyer who purchases direct mail solutions.

I started with this prompt: **What are the pain points for direct mail buyers?**

ChatGPT responded with this:

> *As a direct mail buyer, there are several pain points that you may encounter. Here are some common pain points associated with direct mail:*
>
> *Cost: One of the significant pain points for direct mail buyers is the cost involved in creating and sending direct mail campaigns. Printing, postage, design, and mailing list expenses can add up quickly, especially for large-scale*

campaigns. Balancing the cost and the desired return on investment (ROI) can be a challenge.

Targeting and Personalization: Ensuring that your direct mail reaches the right audience and is personalized to each recipient can be difficult. Acquiring accurate and up-to-date mailing lists and segmenting them appropriately requires time and effort. Lack of targeting and personalization can result in low response rates and wasted resources.

Response Tracking: Unlike digital marketing channels, tracking the response and effectiveness of direct mail campaigns can be more challenging. It can be hard to determine the exact impact of a direct mail piece, including the number of recipients who actually received it, opened it, or took the desired action. This lack of visibility can make it difficult to measure the success of a campaign accurately.

Production and Timelines: Coordinating the production and delivery of direct mail campaigns involves multiple stakeholders, including designers, printers, mail houses, and the postal service. Delays in any of these stages can impact the overall timeline and result in missed deadlines or delivery delays.

Creative and Design Limitations: Direct mail often has physical constraints, such as size, weight, and printing limitations, which can affect the creative possibilities. Designing impactful direct mail pieces that stand out and effectively convey the intended message within these constraints can be a pain point for buyers.

Environmental Concerns: In an era of increasing environmental awareness, the environmental impact of direct mail can be a concern for some buyers. Balancing the effectiveness of direct mail with sustainable practices can be challenging.

Integration with Other Marketing Channels: Coordinating direct mail campaigns with other marketing channels, such as email marketing or social media, can be a pain point. Ensuring consistent messaging and timing across multiple channels requires coordination and strategic planning.

These pain points highlight some of the challenges that direct mail buyers may face. However, many of these challenges can be mitigated through careful planning, strategic targeting, creative design, and the use of advanced tracking and analytics tools.

I scanned the information, picked a pain point, and followed up with this prompt: **Create an email for a direct mail buyer asking for a meeting to discuss ways my company can address this pain point: Response-Tracking: Unlike digital marketing channels, tracking the response and effectiveness of direct mail campaigns can be more challenging. It can be hard to determine the exact impact of a direct mail piece, including the number of recipients who actually received it, opened it, or took the desired action. This lack of visibility can make it difficult to measure the success of a campaign accurately.**

ChatGPT responded with an email.

Subject: Meeting Request: Enhancing Direct Mail Response Tracking for Effective Campaign Analysis

Dear [Prospect's Name],

I hope this email finds you well. My name is [Your Name], and I represent [Your Company], a leading provider of innovative direct mail solutions. I recently came across your challenges with response tracking for direct mail campaigns, and I believe our company can offer valuable solutions to address this pain point.

Tracking the response and effectiveness of direct mail campaigns is a crucial aspect of optimizing your marketing efforts. We understand that the lack of visibility into key metrics, such as the actual reach, open rates, and customer actions, can hinder your ability to accurately measure campaign success and make data-driven decisions.

At [Your Company], we have developed advanced tools and strategies that can significantly enhance the tracking capabilities of your direct mail campaigns. Our expertise in this area can provide you with valuable insights and actionable data to maximize the ROI of your marketing initiatives. We would like to explore these solutions further and discuss how they can be customized to meet your specific needs.

I would like to request a meeting at your convenience to discuss the challenges you are facing and present our innovative response tracking solutions. During the meeting, we can delve deeper into the specific pain points you encounter, showcase our successful case studies, and outline how our technology and methodologies can benefit your organization.

Here are a few topics we can cover during our meeting:

- *Understanding your current response tracking practices and pain points.*
- *Introducing our comprehensive response tracking tools and methodologies.*
- *Demonstrating how our solutions can provide actionable insights and analytics.*
- *Discussing ways to integrate direct mail response tracking with your existing marketing channels for a holistic view of your campaigns.*
- *Customizing our offerings to align with your specific goals and requirements.*
- *Addressing any questions or concerns you may have regarding our solutions.*

Please let me know your availability for a meeting at your earliest convenience. I am flexible and willing to work around your schedule. You can suggest a date and time that suits you best, and we will make the necessary arrangements.

Thank you for considering this meeting request. We look forward to the opportunity to discuss how [Your Company] can empower you to effectively track the response and optimize the success of your direct mail campaigns.

Best regards,

The email I received had over 300 words of body copy—way too long to hold a buyer's interest. My next prompt said, **"Shorten the response above to 100 words or less."**

ChatGPT complied.

Subject: Meeting Request: Enhancing Direct Mail Response Tracking

Dear [Prospect's Name],

I represent [Your Company], specializing in innovative direct mail solutions. We understand the challenges of tracking direct mail responses. Our advanced tools and strategies offer actionable insights and analytics, bridging the gap between digital channels and direct mail. Let's discuss how we can enhance your response tracking and measure campaign success accurately. I request a meeting at your convenience to explore your pain points and showcase our customized solutions. Please suggest a date and time that works for you.

Best regards,

How much time did it take to arrive at this point? **APPROXIMATELY 3 MINUTES!**

The subject line "Enhancing Direct Mail Response Tracking" also performed well enough when I checked it in scoring software.

Would I send this out as it is written? Probably not. Some of it, particularly the meeting request, seems a bit mechanical. And I could improve the subject line based on my sales experience.

To edit, I would paste the ChatGPT copy into Word and clear all the formatting. Then, I would polish and improve, which can be easier than creating an email from scratch.

Adding a preference map (a set of user guidelines) can influence responses and improve results. For example, you could tell ChatGPT you prefer an email with a casual, friendly tone instead of the formal tone automatically generated by the system.

Here are the steps defined by ChatGPT for setting up a preference map.

Creating a preference map for ChatGPT involves a process of defining and specifying the desired behavior and characteristics of the language model. Here's a general outline of the steps involved:

1. *Identify objectives: Determine the primary goals and objectives for using ChatGPT. Consider the context, user needs, and any specific requirements for the conversations with the model.*
2. *Define dimensions: Identify the dimensions or attributes that are important for guiding the model's behavior. These dimensions can include safety, correctness, consistency, specificity, engagement, politeness, and any other relevant aspects.*
3. *Specify preferences: For each dimension, specify the preferred behavior or range. For example, in the safety dimension, you might want to emphasize avoiding offensive or harmful content. In the correctness dimension, you may prioritize accurate and well-supported responses.*

4. *Quantify preferences: Assign quantitative values or ranges to the preferences to create a measurable scale. This step helps in implementing the preferences within the model's configuration.*
5. *Implement preferences: Translate the preference map into a set of guidelines or constraints that can be incorporated into ChatGPT's programming or fine-tuning process. This may involve modifying the model's training data, adjusting the decoding algorithm, or using reinforcement learning techniques.*
6. *Test and iterate: Evaluate the modified ChatGPT against test cases and real-world interactions to ensure that it adheres to the defined preferences. Iterate on the preference map based on feedback and further refinements.*
7. *Continuous improvement: Regularly review and update the preference map as needed to adapt to evolving requirements, user feedback, and ethical considerations.*

It's important to note that the preference map is a tool to guide ChatGPT's behavior, but it may not provide complete control over the model's responses. The complexity and flexibility of language models mean that they can still generate outputs that may not align perfectly with the specified preferences. Therefore, continuous monitoring and iteration are crucial to ensure the desired behavior is maintained.

If you want a call script instead of an email, follow the same basic steps. Just be sure to specify the format (a call script) with a word count between 25 to 40 words.

Like any selling skill, creating emails to get meetings using ChatGPT improves with practice. Try it and see how it works for you.

Once you have a meeting scheduled, ChatGPT continues to be helpful. Let's explore other ways you can use AI during the sales cycle.

CHAPTER EIGHT

PLANNING AND PREPARING FOR MEETINGS

Asking, **"How can ChatGPT help salespeople prepare for meetings with prospects and customers,"** returned this response.

ChatGPT can assist salespeople in preparing for meetings with prospects and customers by providing valuable information, generating ideas, and offering guidance on various aspects of the sales process. Here are some ways in which ChatGPT can help:

Research and Market Insights: ChatGPT can gather relevant information about prospects, companies, industries, and market trends. By analyzing online sources, it can provide insights into the target audience, competitors, and industry challenges. This information can be used to tailor sales pitches and anticipate potential objections.

Message Crafting: Salespeople can collaborate with ChatGPT to refine their value proposition, elevator pitch, and key messages. ChatGPT can offer suggestions, help in structuring *the pitch, and provide feedback on the clarity and effectiveness of the messaging.*

Objection Handling: ChatGPT can simulate common objections that prospects may raise during meetings and assist salespeople in developing effective responses. By brainstorming and role-playing different scenarios, ChatGPT can help refine objection handling techniques, increasing the confidence of the salesperson.

Presentation Assistance: ChatGPT can aid in creating compelling presentations and slide decks by suggesting content, offering design tips, and ensuring the flow of information is logical and engaging. It can also help in adapting the presentation to the specific needs and interests of the prospect or customer.

Competitive Analysis: ChatGPT can assist in researching competitors, understanding their strengths and weaknesses, and identifying unique selling points. By providing competitive insights, it can help salespeople differentiate their offering and position it effectively during the meeting.

Qualifying Questions: Salespeople can collaborate with ChatGPT to develop a list of targeted and insightful questions to ask prospects during meetings. By understanding the prospect's needs, pain points, and goals, salespeople can tailor their solutions and demonstrate value more effectively.

Relationship Building: ChatGPT can offer guidance on building rapport, establishing trust, and fostering meaningful relationships with prospects and customers. It can provide suggestions on personalizing conversations, finding common ground, and maintaining a customer-centric approach.

Follow-up Strategies: After the meeting, ChatGPT can help in strategizing follow-up actions, such as crafting personalized follow-up emails, scheduling next steps, or addressing any specific concerns or requests that arose during the meeting.

It's important to note that while ChatGPT can provide valuable insights and suggestions, it should be used as a tool to support the salesperson's expertise and judgment. Human intuition, empathy, and adaptability are crucial in the sales process, and ChatGPT can complement these qualities by offering information and generating ideas.

While this information contains good points, it is broad-based and general. Sometimes, it makes sense to use an answer as a starting point and narrow it down through follow-up queries.

In other cases, it makes more sense to think outside ChatGPT for a better way to approach the problem. After reading this response, I decided to start from a different point. I took a few minutes, jotted down my thoughts on what I wanted to know, and used that to build a set of actionable steps for planning sales calls.

Prompts to Plan a Call

Think of a buyer you plan to meet, and use ChatGPT to plan the call.

- Start with a question to identify pain points, problems, and challenges. Example: What problems and challenges do buyers (in the industry at a company category) have related to (the product or service you sell)?
- Scan the information. Create a follow-up question directly referencing the product or service you want to sell and how it helps buyers solve a project or overcome a challenge. Tip: ChatGPT provides better information when you are specific and include relevant context. Answers often improve when you paste in benefits or descriptions before asking questions.
- Use the response to ask for a list of discovery questions. Example: What questions should I ask about (the product or service you sell) to find out if a buyer has problems or is seeking improvements in (a process or outcome related to what you want to sell)?

This sequence gives you plenty of information for planning a call. ChatGPT can also turn the information into an agenda when you type, ***"Turn this information into an agenda."***

Let's look at an example. Murial sells IT consulting and support services to mid-size enterprises with between 50 to 100 employees. Next week, she has a call with Stuart Benson, the CFO at LuxLawn Furniture, a lawn furniture manufacturing company. Stuart is responsible for IT and data security at his company and uses outside consultants for these services.

Murial started her ChatGPT session by asking: **What problems and challenges do buyers of IT Services and IT consulting have related to finding the right IT solutions and consulting partner?**

ChatGPT responded:

Buyers of IT services and IT consulting often face several problems and challenges when trying to find the right IT solutions and consulting partner. Here are some common issues they may encounter:

1. *Identifying their exact requirements: Buyers may struggle to clearly define their IT needs and requirements. They may have a general idea of the problem they want to solve or the outcome they want to achieve, but translating that into specific IT solutions can be challenging.*
2. *Understanding available technologies: The technology landscape is constantly evolving, and buyers may find it difficult to keep up with the latest trends and advancements. They may lack the knowledge and expertise to evaluate different technologies and determine which ones are most suitable for their needs.*
3. *Navigating the market: The IT services and consulting market can be crowded and confusing. There are numerous vendors and providers offering a wide range of services, making it challenging for buyers to differentiate between them and identify the most suitable partner.*

4. *Assessing vendor capabilities: Buyers need to evaluate the capabilities and expertise of potential IT services and consulting partners. They may struggle to assess a vendor's track record, industry experience, technical skills, and the quality of their past work. Lack of objective criteria can make this evaluation process even more difficult.*

5. *Alignment with business goals: Buyers must ensure that the chosen IT solutions and consulting partner align with their overall business goals and strategies. Achieving this alignment requires a deep understanding of the organization's objectives and how technology can support them.*

6. *Budget constraints: IT services and consulting can be costly, and buyers often have budget limitations. Balancing cost considerations with the need for high-quality solutions and reliable partners can be a significant challenge.*

7. *Managing risk: Implementing new IT solutions or engaging with a consulting partner involves inherent risks. Buyers need to assess and manage these risks effectively, such as data security, project delays, or potential disruptions to business operations.*

8. *Scalability and future-proofing: Buyers need to consider the scalability and long-term viability of the IT solutions and consulting partner. They should anticipate future growth and technological advancements to ensure that the chosen solutions can accommodate evolving needs.*

9. *Communication and collaboration: Effective communication and collaboration between the buyer and the IT services/consulting partner are vital for successful outcomes. Challenges may arise in terms of aligning expectations, maintaining regular communication, and fostering a collaborative working relationship.*
10. *Change management: Implementing new IT solutions often requires change within the organization. Buyers may encounter resistance to change, employee training needs, and the need to manage the transition effectively to ensure smooth adoption of the new technology.*

Addressing these challenges often requires a systematic approach, thorough research, and careful evaluation of potential IT services and consulting partners. Buyers may consider seeking recommendations, conducting in-depth interviews, and reviewing case studies or testimonials to make more informed decisions.

Murial scanned the answers. She decided to focus the call on the challenges of finding an IT partner aligned with the company's business goals and objectives. She asked: **"Why does it help a lawn care furniture manufacturer to find an IT partner and consultant who will invest time in learning about lawn care furniture manufacturing?"**

ChatGPT responded:

It is beneficial for the CFO of a lawn care furniture manufacturer to find an IT partner and consultant who is willing to invest time in learning about lawn care furniture manufacturing for several reasons:

1. Understanding business processes: By familiarizing themselves with the lawn care furniture industry and manufacturing operations, the IT partner can gain a deeper understanding of the specific challenges, workflows, and requirements unique to the business. This knowledge allows them to develop IT solutions that are tailored to the company's needs, improving efficiency and effectiveness.

2. Industry-specific expertise: A consultant who invests time in learning about the lawn care business can bring valuable industry-specific knowledge to the table. They can provide insights and best practices based on their understanding of the market, regulatory compliance, and operational considerations within the lawn care furniture industry.

3. Customization of IT solutions: Lawn care furniture manufacturing may have specific software requirements, data management needs, or integration challenges. By investing time in learning about the business, the IT partner can customize their solutions to address these unique requirements. This customization ensures that the technology solutions align with the company's processes and can maximize operational efficiency.

4. Identifying pain points and opportunities: A consultant who understands the lawn care furniture business can identify pain points, bottlenecks, and

areas for improvement more effectively. They can offer innovative IT solutions to address these challenges and leverage technology to capitalize on growth opportunities specific to the industry. This industry-focused perspective can lead to better strategic decision-making and help the CFO drive business growth.

5. *Effective communication and collaboration: When the IT partner invests time in learning about the lawn care furniture business, they can communicate and collaborate more effectively with the CFO and other stakeholders. They can speak the same language, understand the industry-specific terminology, and engage in meaningful discussions about business goals and IT requirements. This alignment enhances collaboration and ensures that the IT partner becomes a true partner in driving the business forward.*

6. *Long-term partnership: Investing time in understanding the lawn care furniture business demonstrates a commitment from the IT partner to build a long-term partnership. Rather than providing generic IT services, they are willing to go the extra mile to understand the unique challenges and opportunities in the industry. This commitment fosters trust, strengthens the relationship, and promotes a collaborative approach to problem-solving.*

> *In summary, an IT partner and consultant who invests time in learning about the lawn care furniture business and manufacturing can provide customized solutions, industry-specific expertise, and better collaboration. This understanding enables the CFO to leverage technology effectively, address specific challenges, and drive the company's growth and success.*

After scanning the responses, Murial selected the third point and entered this prompt: **Based on this information, 'Customization of IT solutions: Lawn care furniture manufacturing may have specific software requirements, data management needs, or integration challenges. By investing time in learning about the business, the IT partner can customize their solutions to address these unique requirements. This customization ensures that the technology solutions align with the company's processes and can maximize operational efficiency,' what discovery questions should a salesperson ask the CFO in a sales call?**

ChatGPT responded:

> *During a sales call, a salesperson can ask the following discovery questions to understand the lawn care furniture manufacturer's specific software requirements, data management needs, and integration challenges:*
>
> 1. *What are your current software systems and tools used for managing various aspects of your lawn care furniture manufacturing operations?*

2. Are there any specific functionalities or features that your current software systems lack, hindering your operational efficiency or growth?

3. What are the key pain points or challenges you face in terms of data management within your lawn care furniture manufacturing processes?

4. How do you currently handle data integration between different systems or departments within your organization?

5. Are there any specific regulatory or compliance requirements that your software solutions need to adhere to in the lawn care industry?

6. Can you describe any unique processes or workflows specific to your lawn care furniture manufacturing operations that might require customization or specialized software solutions?

7. What are your goals and expectations for implementing new IT solutions within your lawn care furniture manufacturing operations?

8. How do you envision technology improving your operational efficiency, productivity, or cost management in the context of your business?

9. Are there any future expansion plans or growth strategies that need to be considered when implementing new IT solutions?

10. How do you currently track and analyze key performance indicators (KPIs) related to your lawn care furniture manufacturing operations, and what kind of reporting and analytics capabilities do you require?

> 11. *How do different departments or teams within your organization collaborate and share data or information? Are there any bottlenecks or challenges in this regard?*
>
> 12. *Are there any specific industry standards or best practices that you would like to integrate into your IT solutions?*
>
> *These questions aim to uncover the specific requirements and challenges the lawn care furniture manufacturer faces, allowing the salesperson to tailor their proposed solutions and demonstrate how their offerings can address those needs effectively. It enables the salesperson to position themselves as a consultant and trusted advisor, highlighting the value of customization and alignment with the company's unique processes.*

Murial's ChatGPT planning session took about 10 minutes and provided her with plenty of ammunition for her sales call.

Notice that Murial's prompts are specific. For example, when she asked about discovery questions, she included, **"What discovery questions should a salesperson ask the CFO in a sales call?"** She let ChatGPT know she was looking for a response reflecting her role as a sales rep and focused on the buyer's industry.

After collecting information, Murial asked ChatGPT to create an agenda for a 30-minute meeting. The system complied with an overload of details, but it gave Mural this starting point.

Agenda for a 30-Minute Sales Call: Customized IT Solutions for Lawn Care Furniture Manufacturing

 I. *Introduction and rapport building (5 minutes)*

  A. *Greet the CFO and establish a friendly and professional tone.*

  B. *Briefly introduce yourself and your company.*

  C. *Engage in small talk to build rapport.*

 II. *Understanding the current software landscape (5 minutes)*

  A. *Ask about the lawn care furniture manufacturer's current software systems and tools used for managing their operations.*

  B. *Inquire about any limitations or pain points they experience with their existing software solutions.*

  C. *Listen attentively and take notes to identify areas for improvement.*

 III. *Data management and integration challenges (5 minutes)*

  A. *Explore the CFO's perspective on data management within their lawn care furniture manufacturing processes.*

  B. *Ask about any specific data integration challenges they face between systems or departments.*

  C. *Seek information on their regulatory or compliance requirements related to data management.*

IV. Customization and alignment with processes (5 minutes)
   A. Probe into any unique processes or workflows that require customized software solutions.
   B. Inquire about the CFO's expectations and specific requirements for aligning technology with their manufacturing processes.
   C. Emphasize the value of customization in maximizing operational efficiency.
V. Goals and expectations (5 minutes)
   A. Understand the CFO's goals and expectations for implementing new IT solutions within their lawn care furniture manufacturing operations.
   B. Discuss how technology can address their pain points, improve productivity, and support their growth strategies.
   C. Encourage the CFO to share their vision for technology-driven improvements.

VI. Reporting, analytics, and collaboration (5 minutes)
   A. Explore how the CFO currently tracks and analyzes key performance indicators (KPIs) within their manufacturing operations.
   B. Inquire about reporting and analytics needs and any challenges in collaboration and data sharing between teams.
   C. Highlight how customized IT solutions can enhance reporting capabilities and facilitate seamless collaboration.

VII. *Future expansion and considerations (5 minutes)*

    A. *Discuss the CFO's future expansion plans or growth strategies that need to be considered when implementing new IT solutions.*

    B. *Explore scalability and flexibility requirements to accommodate future needs.*

    C. *Address how the proposed IT solutions can support their long-term objectives.*

VIII. *Summary and next steps (5 minutes)*

    A. *Summarize the key points discussed during the call, emphasizing the customization and alignment with their unique requirements.*

    B. *Address any remaining questions or concerns the CFO may have.*

    C. *Propose the next steps, such as a follow-up meeting, product demonstration, or providing additional information tailored to their needs.*

IX. *Closing and thank you (1 minute)*

    A. *Express appreciation for the CFO's time and the opportunity to discuss their IT needs.*

    B. *Confirm the next steps and provide contact information for further communication.*

Note: The time allocations provided are approximate and can be adjusted based on the flow of the conversation and the importance of certain topics to the CFO.

Murial copied the agenda, pasted it into a Word document, removed ChatGPT's formatting, and deleted everything she viewed as unnecessary. She added her client's name, title, and company at the top, along with the meeting date. At the bottom, she added her contact information.

A few days before the meeting, she emailed Peter, told him she looked forward to meeting him, and attached the agenda, asking him to let her know if he wanted to cover something she hadn't mentioned.

Peter got Murial's message, looked at the agenda, and was impressed. Within minutes of receiving her email, he sent back an email response. "Agenda looks great and looking forward to meeting you too."

Pluses and Minuses

Murial is an experienced sales pro who has sold IT consulting and solutions for seven years. ChatGPT doesn't replace her hard-earned knowledge or sales expertise. Most of the time, it reinforces what she already knows.

However, ChatGPT's responses can usually be quickly skimmed, and the information can be used to speed up call planning several ways:

- A prompt asking about the basics of a specific industry helps you sound knowledgeable to potential buyers.
- Reviewing lists of common problems and pain points brings knowledge to the forefront of your mind, ensuring you are better prepared for a call and ready to link the benefits of your solutions to the buyer's challenges.
- Creating a list of discovery questions can offer new possibilities for uncovering information.

- You can also use ChatGPT to create information to be shared in the meeting, such as executive briefs, solution summaries, case studies, and presentations.

Let's look at other types of information that can help you improve sales calls.

CHAPTER NINE

CREATING RELEVANT INFORMATION FOR SALES CALLS

Chat GPT can help you produce materials to use in a sales call, such as:

- Executive summaries.
- Case studies.
- Presentations.
- Sell sheets about products, services, and solutions.

Before you invest time in creating sales materials using AI, check with executives at your company to be sure you are following the correct protocols, policies, and permissions.

Executive Summaries

An executive summary or brief contains one to three pages of high-level information. It often is used to outline a problem and recommend a solution. Sometimes, the summary includes a budget or a budget range. It is not the same as a proposal or quote because even if it contains pricing information, it doesn't represent a contractual offer.

To use ChatGPT to create an executive summary, you need to write a query that provides all the necessary details and presents all relevant details to create a summary with some or all the following sections:

- Introduction, defining the current situation.
- Your proposed solution.
- Any other relevant information, such as timelines or budgets.
- Expected outcome.
- Closing.

You can do this by inputting a prompt covering all the information or working in sections. I have tried both and find working in sections is easier and usually gets better results.

Here are some tips for writing prompts for the sections.

Section	Prompt Tips
Introduction	• Start with a general description of the customer's business. Copying information off their website or a company page on LinkedIn will work in your prompt. • Explain the problem with relevant details.

Solution	• Explain your recommended solution.
	• Explain why your solution will fix the problem.
Other Information	• Provide any other pertinent information, such as budgets or timelines.
Expected Outcome	• Provide a summary of the positive outcome.
	• Include details about benefits.
Closing	• Include why you are the right partner to help the customer solve their problem.
	• Mention any next steps.
	• Thank the customer for the opportunity to present the information.

Proof, add a company logo, and fill in missing details, like the client's contact information, a date, and your name and title, and you are ready to go!

Case Studies

ChatGPT can save you time if you want to organize and present information as a case study or success story. Generally, this format includes the following:

- Title.
- A summary of the situation and outcome.
- Background information, including details about the client.

- An explanation of the client's challenge with any relevant information related to the client's decision-making process.
- Explanation of the solution, including what it was, why it was selected, and how you were chosen.
- The outcome, including a testimonial if the client is willing to provide one.

If you want to name a company, you may need permission to include that information.

You can still tell the story when customers don't want to be named. Stick to generalities and use top-level descriptors such as "a major national manufacturer" or "a long-time customer."

Once more, I recommend working in sections, using these tips to write your prompts.

Section	Prompt Tips
Title	<ul><li>Start with, "Give me a title for a case study about . . ."</li><li>Explain the topic.</li><li>After writing the case study, you can paste the copy into ChatGPT and ask for title suggestions if you want more options.</li></ul>
Summary	<ul><li>Include a few details and ask for a summary.</li></ul>
The Challenge	<ul><li>Outline the client's problem and pain points.</li></ul>

	• Explain what the client had tried to eliminate the problem. • Include any relevant details about the client's decision-making process. For example, if the purchaser was asked to find a solution, include that information.
The Solution	• Provide details about the solution. • Include what the solution was, why it was selected, and why you were chosen as the solution provider.
Outcome	• What was the outcome once your solution was implemented? • Provide details about positive benefits, higher productivity, cost savings, increased ROI, or improved profitability.

Add any supporting charts, pictures, or details. Proof and include your company logo, website, and your contact information. If you must have your case study reviewed by an individual or department before using it, follow your company's protocols.

Presentations

I asked ChatGPT, *"What makes sales calls that include a presentation more interesting than a basic conversation?"*

The system responded:

Sales calls that include a presentation can be more interesting than basic conversations for several reasons:

1. *Visual Appeal: Presentations often involve visual aids such as slides, graphs, or product demonstrations. These visual elements can capture the attention of the listener and make the sales call more engaging. Visuals can help illustrate key points, showcase product features, and create a memorable impression.*

2. *Structure and Organization: Presentations provide a structured format that helps guide the conversation and ensure important information is covered. This can make the sales call more efficient and effective, as the presenter can systematically present the benefits, features, and value propositions of the product or service. A well-organized presentation can keep the listener focused and prevent information from being overlooked or forgotten.*

3. *Information Retention: Studies have shown that people tend to remember information better when it is presented visually or through a combination of visual and auditory cues. By incorporating visual elements into the sales call, such as charts, images, or videos, the presenter can enhance the listener's understanding and retention of the key messages.*

4. *Engagement and Interaction: A presentation can create opportunities for interaction and engagement between the salesperson and the prospect. For example, the presenter can ask questions, encourage participation, or seek feedback during the*

> *presentation. This active involvement can make the sales call more dynamic, encourage dialogue, and build rapport with the prospect.*
>
> 5. *Professionalism and Credibility: Presenting information in a structured and visually appealing manner can enhance the perception of professionalism and expertise. It demonstrates that the salesperson has prepared for the call, understands the product or service, and is committed to delivering a persuasive message. This can instill confidence in the prospect and increase the perceived credibility of the salesperson and the offering.*
>
> *It's important to note that while presentations can make sales calls more interesting, they should be tailored to the needs and preferences of the prospect. Some individuals may prefer a more conversational approach, so it's essential to adapt the sales style accordingly and strike a balance between presentation and active listening.*

ChatGPT can provide ideas for presentations. It can turn notes, queries, and research into slide series and offer suggestions on visuals.

Here are prompt tips for creating a presentation.

Action	Prompt Tips
Presentation Length and Title	• Start by defining the length of the presentation.

	• Set a limit on the number of slides. • If you have a title, include it, or ChatGPT can provide a suggestion.
Define the Audience.	• Write a statement defining the audience and anything relevant to their pain points.
Define Important Information	• State what you want to explain or sell. • Include key points related to benefits, your value, and how to eliminate the audience's pain points.
Outcome	• Provide details about the outcome. • Include proof or a testimonial if available.
Next Steps and Closing	• Include details about the next steps. • Thank the customer for their time.

Here is an example of how I used ChatGPT to put together a presentation for a customer who was considering my company for training on sales territory management.

I started by writing a prompt outlining the presentation requirements that said: ***Create a 30-minute presentation. The topic for the presentation is "An Overview of Territory Management Sales Training." The audience is the***

Executive Vice President in charge of operations who oversees the sales team.

The presentation should include the following:

- *What is Territory Management?*
- *Why does territory management benefit a company?*
- *How do you organize a Territory Management Plan?*
- *What should salespeople be trained on to execute a territory management plan effectively?*
- *If a sales team is trained in territory management, what are the benefits to the company?*
- *Conclusion.*

Here is the response:

Title: An Overview of Territory Management Sales Training

Slide 1: Introduction

- *Greet the audience and introduce yourself*
- *State the topic: "An Overview of Territory Management Sales Training"*
- *Mention the agenda and duration of the presentation*

Slide 2: What is Territory Management?

- *Define territory management: The strategic process of dividing a market into specific geographic areas to assign sales representatives and optimize sales efforts.*

- *Explain how territory management provides structure and organization to the sales team's activities.*

Slide 3: Why does territory management benefit a company?

- *Increased sales productivity: Salespeople can focus on specific territories, allowing them to build deeper relationships with customers and increase sales.*
- *Efficient resource allocation: Territory management helps allocate resources, time, and effort based on market potential, ensuring optimal utilization.*
- *Enhanced customer satisfaction: Dedicated sales reps provide personalized attention and tailored solutions, leading to improved customer satisfaction and loyalty.*

Slide 4: How do you organize a Territory Management Plan?

- *Define the key components of a territory management plan:*
- *Define territories: Identify geographic areas based on factors like market size, customer density, and sales potential.*
- *Assign sales reps: Match salespeople with territories based on their skills, experience, and product knowledge.*
- *Set objectives: Establish clear goals and targets for each territory to align sales efforts with business objectives.*

- *Develop a routing plan: Determine the most efficient routes for salespeople to cover their assigned territories.*
- *Monitor and evaluate: Implement processes to track progress, measure performance, and make necessary adjustments.*

Slide 5: What should salespeople be trained on to execute a territory management plan effectively?

- *Product knowledge: Understanding the features, benefits, and value propositions of the company's products or services.*
- *Sales techniques: Training on effective sales strategies, negotiation skills, objection handling, and closing deals.*
- *Time management: Techniques to prioritize tasks, manage schedules, and maximize productivity.*
- *Customer relationship management: Training on building and maintaining strong customer relationships, including active listening and effective communication.*

Slide 6: If a sales team is trained in territory management, what are the benefits to the company?

- *Increased sales revenue: Trained salespeople can identify and capitalize on opportunities within their territories, leading to improved sales performance.*
- *Better customer satisfaction: Sales reps equipped with territory management training can provide*

superior customer service, leading to increased loyalty and repeat business.

- *Improved efficiency and effectiveness: Training enables salespeople to optimize their time, prioritize tasks, and make strategic decisions within their territories.*
- *Enhanced teamwork and collaboration: Territory management training promotes a coordinated approach, fostering collaboration among sales team members.*

Slide 7: Conclusion

- *Recap the main points covered in the presentation:*
- *Definition and importance of territory management*
- *Benefits to the company*
- *Organizing a territory management plan*
- *Training requirements for salespeople*
- *Benefits of territory management training*
- *Emphasize the potential impact of implementing territory management sales training on the company's overall sales performance and customer satisfaction.*
- *Thank the audience for their time and open the floor for questions.*

Note: Adapt the presentation content and add visual aids such as charts, graphs, or examples to enhance understanding and engage the audience effectively.

I took one more step and asked ChatGPT to give me suggestions for presentation visuals for the main slides.

ChatGPT came back with this:

Certainly! Here are some recommended visuals for the main slides of your presentation:

Slide 2: What is Territory Management?

- *A visual representation of a map with different territories highlighted, showcasing how the market is divided geographically.*
- *Icons or images representing sales representatives assigned to specific territories, highlighting the concept of dedicated coverage.*
- *Slide 3: Why does territory management benefit a company?*
- *A bar chart comparing sales productivity before and after implementing territory management, illustrating the increase in sales achieved.*
- *A pie chart showcasing the allocation of resources (time, effort, and budget) before and after territory management, highlighting the improved efficiency.*

Slide 4: How do you organize a Territory Management Plan?

- *An infographic or flowchart illustrating the step-by-step process of organizing a territory management plan, showing the sequence of defining territories, assigning sales reps, setting objectives, developing routing plans, and monitoring and evaluating.*

Slide 5: What should salespeople be trained on to execute a territory management plan effectively?

- *A slide with bullet points or icons representing the key training areas, such as product knowledge, sales techniques, time management, and customer relationship management.*

Slide 6: If a sales team is trained in territory management, what are the benefits to the company?

- *A comparison slide showing the increase in sales revenue with territory management, represented by a line graph or an upward arrow.*
- *A visual representation of a satisfied customer, such as a smiling face or a thumbs-up icon, highlighting improved customer satisfaction.*

Slide 7: Conclusion

- *A slide summarizing the main points covered in the presentation using a bullet-point list or a visual summary.*
- *A closing image or a thank-you slide with your contact information and company logo.*

Remember, visuals should complement your content and make it easier for the audience to understand and remember key points. Feel free to adapt and customize these suggestions based on your presentation style and available resources.

You now have a starting point, but the copy generated by ChatGPT must still be placed into a presentation format like PowerPoint, Keynote, or Google Slides. Design templates are available in these solutions, as well as other programs like Canva or Prezi.

Sell Sheets

Even when your company has a strong marketing team and lots of collateral, there may be times when you wish you had a specific sell sheet to promote a product, service, or solution.

Sell sheets are information summaries highlighting key product benefits and features. The purpose of the sell sheet is to persuade buyers to take the next step, which could be asking for more in-depth information or requesting a pricing proposal.

It's helpful to know how to create sell sheets when:

- You have a brand-new solution to sell and don't have any marketing collateral.
- You need customer-specific support materials to cross-sell or up-sell a single service.
- You are looking for a fresh way to present a long-standing product or service.

I asked ChatGPT, *"What are the elements in a product or service sell sheet?"*

The system responded with this information:

> *A product or service sell sheet typically includes several key elements to effectively showcase and promote the offering. While the specific elements may vary based on the nature of*

the product or service and the target audience, here are some common components found in a sell sheet:

- *Headline or Tagline: A catchy and attention-grabbing statement that communicates the main benefit or unique selling proposition of the product or service.*
- *Product or Service Description: A brief and compelling overview of what the product or service is, highlighting its main features, functions, and benefits. This section should focus on the value it provides to the customer.*
- *Visuals: High-quality images, illustrations, or product mockups that visually represent the offering. Visuals should be appealing, informative, and help customers understand what the product or service looks like or how it works.*
- *Key Features: A list or concise description of the most important features or characteristics of the product or service. These features should be presented in a clear and easy-to-read format, highlighting what sets the offering apart from competitors.*
- *Benefits: Emphasize the advantages and benefits that customers can expect to gain by using the product or service. Focus on how it solves a problem, saves time or money, improves efficiency, enhances quality, or meets specific needs.*
- *Pricing and Packages: Clearly state the pricing structure, different package options, or any special offers or discounts available. This information helps potential customers understand the cost and value of the product or service.*

- *Testimonials or Customer Reviews: Including positive feedback or testimonials from satisfied customers can build trust and credibility. Quotes or ratings that highlight the positive experiences of existing customers can reinforce the value proposition of the product or service.*
- *Contact Information: Provide relevant contact details, such as a phone number, email address, website, or social media handles, through which potential customers can reach out for more information or to make a purchase.*
- *Call-to-Action (CTA): Clearly state the desired action you want potential customers to take, such as "Call now," "Visit our website," or "Request a demo." A well-placed and compelling CTA encourages readers to take the next step.*
- *Branding and Design Elements: Incorporate consistent branding elements, such as your company logo, colors, and fonts, to reinforce brand recognition and create a professional and cohesive look.*

Remember, the content and design of a sell sheet should be concise, visually appealing, and tailored to the needs and preferences of your target audience. It should present the most important information in an easily digestible format, capturing the reader's attention and motivating them to engage further with your product or service.

Here are prompt tips for creating a sell sheet.

Action	Prompt Tips
Product/Service/Solution Name and Value Proposition Statement	• Name the product/service/solution. • Tell ChatGPT what the product does, who it helps, and why.
Sell the Benefits	• Write a list of the benefits. • Ask ChatGPT to provide an introductory paragraph and three to five key benefits.
Call Out the Product Features.	• List the product's traits or attributes that deliver value to your customers and differentiate your product in the market.
Call to Action	• Define the next step. • Ask for a call to action to persuade the buyer to take the next step.

I used this framework to create a prompt to write a sell sheet for the sales training on territory management that read: *Create a sell sheet for a sales training session. The title of the training session is "Territory Management Sales Training." This 4-hour sales training session provides new sales representatives with all the fundamentals they need to know to plan how to cover the accounts in a sales territory. The benefits of the session include:*

- *Customized for your company.*
- *Practical information on how to map a route to see all accounts in your territory.*
- *It covers time management, assessing account business potential, and who you should see when you visit an account.*

Features include:

- *Handouts.*
- *Professional presentation.*
- *Interactive discussion.*
- *Worksheets to develop a territory plan.*
- *Practical information that can be applied immediately.*
- *Training can be conducted in person or as an online session.*

The next step is asking for a proposal. The call to action is telling the decision-maker to request a proposal for a customized session.

ChatGPT responded with this copy:

[Header] Territory Management Sales Training

Unlock Your Sales Potential

[Description] Are your sales representatives equipped to conquer their territories? Empower your team with our comprehensive 4-hour training session on Territory Management. Designed for new sales representatives, this training provides essential fundamentals to effectively plan and cover accounts within a sales territory.

[Benefits] Customized for Your Company: Tailored to your specific needs and industry, our training session ensures relevance and maximum impact for your team.

- *Map Your Route to Success: Learn practical strategies to map out an optimized route, ensuring you reach all accounts in your territory efficiently and effectively.*
- *Master Time Management: Discover proven techniques for prioritizing tasks and managing time to maximize productivity and results.*
- *Unlock Account Potential: Gain insights into assessing the business potential of each account and identifying key decision-makers to focus your efforts and boost sales.*

[Features]

- *Comprehensive Materials: Receive comprehensive handouts and resources that serve as valuable references long after the training session ends.*
- *Professional Presentation: Experience a dynamic and engaging training environment led by our experienced sales trainers who understand your industry.*
- *Interactive Discussions: Engage in lively discussions, share experiences, and learn from fellow sales professionals to enhance your learning experience.*
- *Territory Planning Worksheets: Put theory into practice with our practical worksheets designed to guide you in developing a strategic territory plan tailored to your specific needs.*

- *Immediate Application: Benefit from actionable insights and real-world techniques that you can apply immediately to enhance your sales performance.*
- *Flexible Training Options: Choose between in-person sessions for hands-on learning or online sessions for convenience and accessibility.*

[Call-to-Action] Ready to unleash your sales team's potential? Request a customized proposal for our Territory Management Sales Training session today. Equip your representatives with the skills and strategies they need to dominate their territories and drive sales success. Contact us now to take the first step toward unlocking greater sales achievements.

[Contact Information] Phone: [Phone Number] Email: [Email Address] Website: [Website URL]

Keep in mind that ChatGPT can help you develop the copy for a sell sheet, but it must still be presented to the buyer in a professional document. One option for adding polish is dropping the copy into a customizable flyer template in Microsoft Word. Once more, use good judgment on whether you need internal approval for your sell sheet before showing it to a buyer.

Beyond creating information to present in a sales meeting, ChatGPT can also support follow-up strategies. Let's look at that next.

CHAPTER TEN

STAND-OUT FOLLOW-UP STRATEGIES

Occasionally, sales pros experience the one-call close. When this happens, you connect with the buyer, pitch your solution, and get an order—all in one sales call. Celebrate when this happens because most B2B sales are only made after you follow up and make multiple calls.

In this chapter, we'll break down a common scenario to examine how ChatGPT can help you develop and execute a follow-up strategy to close more deals.

Let's say you had a significant meeting with a potential buyer named Sandra, and it was fantastic! Sandra was unhappy with her current vendor and had a significant pain point she wanted to eliminate. You presented your company's solution, and Sandra's eyes lit up. She demonstrated an active interest and asked the questions prospects ask when they are serious about buying.

You talked for an hour and would have happily continued the conversation. Unfortunately, Sandra had to attend another meeting. She promised you would talk again soon.

You left Sandra's office, walked to your car, climbed in, and headed back to your office, thinking about the meeting. Even though it went well, you still had miles to travel before Sandra handed you a signed purchase order. And it was likely she would talk to at least one of your competitors before purchasing.

To win, you needed a strong follow-up strategy to stay top-of-mind and set yourself apart from your competitors.

Let's explore ways that ChatGPT can help you follow up and make the sale.

Include Meeting Notes with Your Thank-You Email

It is standard procedure to send an email after a meeting to thank a prospective customer for seeing you. Less common is to send the customer an executive summary containing your meeting notes.

Sending meeting notes is a smart follow-up strategy, particularly when you are working on a major deal because:

- You look professional and provide proof you are a good listener.
- It sets you apart from competitors early on unless they also send meeting notes, and most competitors won't take the extra step.

- You can reinforce your value proposition within your notes, presenting information in a way that makes you a logical choice.

ChatGPT is your virtual assistant, turning scribbled notes into a cohesive and professional summary.

If your notes are handwritten, the first step is to put them into a typed document. The fastest and easiest way to do this is by opening a word-processing program on your phone and voice-recording your notes so they can be copied and pasted into ChatGPT with appropriate instructions.

If your sales calls take place online, you may want to investigate AI note-taking solutions to use in conjunction with technology. An online search or asking ChatGPT can find suggestions for free and paid options.

Follow-Up Emails

ChatGPT can help you craft a series of short follow-up emails after your initial meeting. Many of the principles about writing emails discussed in Chapters Six and Seven can also be applied to follow-up emails.

In a perfect world, when a buyer agrees to take the next step and when you send an email requesting another meeting, the buyer promptly agrees. Unfortunately, we often don't sell in perfect situations, and the response may not come as quickly as you hoped.

Does this mean the buyer has lost interest? Possibly, but there are other reasons why the buyer may not respond instantly. You don't win the race by quitting too soon, so you need an extended follow-up strategy that communicates you are ready to help while continuing to educate buyers on your company's value proposition.

ChatGPT can help you create a series of short emails for follow-up purposes, ending with an appropriate call-to-action.

Here are tips for prompts to ask ChatGPT to craft a series of follow-up emails.

Action	Prompt Tips
State what you want to create.	• Define how many emails you want to send and the goal of the emails. • Define the number of words in each email. I recommend setting a limit of 100 to 150 words. • Define the tone of the emails as friendly and professional.
Provide details on points discussed in your initial meeting.	• Outline pain points or the problem to solve. • Mention benefits you wish to reaffirm. • Mention the expected outcome if the buyer chooses you as a vendor.
Next steps and call-to-action.	• Ask to include a call-to-action requesting the buyer take the next step.

Previously, I used ChatGPT to create information related to a sales training session on territory management. Let's assume I had my initial meeting with a potential client. In that meeting, we discussed the training session and why my company was the right choice for a partner. However, the prospect wanted time to think about the information I shared and asked me to follow up in two weeks. I set a reminder in my calendar and used ChatGPT.

I asked the system to create three follow-up emails. Why three? I knew from personal experience selling sales training that interested prospects generally made buying decisions in 10 to 30 days.

However, even interested buyers don't always respond to the first email sent after a meeting. When you write follow-up emails from scratch, creating multiple emails involves a significant time investment.

ChatGPT can write three emails in less than a minute. If the buyer ignores your first email, grab the next one in your sequence and fire it off.

I used this prompt to ask ChatGPT to write three follow-up emails to sell sales training about territory management: ***Create a series of three emails to follow up an initial sales call where the buyer was interested in buying sales training on territory management. The body copy of the emails is 100 to 120 words long. The tone is professional and friendly.***

Points we discussed in the sales meeting include:

- *The reasons to train on this topic – more opportunities, better time management, and higher revenues.*
- *The current salespeople lack experience managing a territory, so opportunities are lost because many accounts do not receive enough attention.*
- *The benefits of training include a professional presentation, handouts, and practical information that can be applied immediately.*

At the end of the email, include a call to action asking the buyer to meet again to discuss a proposal.

ChatGPT responded with this:

Email 1:

Subject: Recap and Next Steps for Territory Management Training

Dear [Buyer's Name],

I hope this email finds you well. I wanted to take a moment to thank you for our insightful discussion earlier regarding your team's need for territory management training. As we discussed, implementing this training program can bring about several significant benefits, including increased opportunities, improved time management, and ultimately higher revenues.

Based on our conversation, it's clear that your salespeople would greatly benefit from enhancing their territory management skills. Without proper experience, valuable accounts are often overlooked, resulting in missed

---

opportunities. Our training program offers a comprehensive solution to address this challenge.

I would like to propose a follow-up meeting to discuss our customized training solution further. Please let me know your availability, and we can arrange a convenient time. I look forward to continuing our conversation.

Best regards, [Your Name]

Email 2:

Subject: Tailored Training for Effective Territory Management

Dear [Buyer's Name],

I hope this email finds you well. Following our previous conversation about the importance of territory management training, I wanted to reiterate the benefits our program can bring to your team. Our training sessions offer a professional presentation, comprehensive handouts, and practical information that can be immediately applied in the field.

By equipping your salespeople with the necessary skills and techniques, we can help them better manage their territories, ensuring that no accounts go overlooked. This will lead to a significant increase in opportunities and ultimately drive higher revenues for your organization.

I would be delighted to meet with you again to present a detailed proposal tailored to your specific needs. Please let me know a convenient time to continue our discussion. I look forward to the opportunity to work with you and your team.

Best regards, [Your Name]

Email 3:

Subject: Taking the Next Steps: Proposal Discussion

Dear [Buyer's Name],

I hope this email finds you well. Thank you for expressing interest in our territory management training program. After our initial conversation, it is clear that your sales team can greatly benefit from the professional development and enhanced skills our program offers.

To help you understand the full scope of our training, I would like to propose a follow-up meeting where we can discuss the detailed proposal we have prepared for your consideration. This proposal outlines the customized training sessions, timelines, and investment required.

I believe our program can make a significant impact on your team's performance, leading to increased opportunities and ultimately higher revenues. Please let me know your availability, and I will gladly schedule a meeting at your convenience.

Thank you once again for considering our services. I look forward to meeting with you and exploring how we can contribute to your team's success.

Best regards, [Your Name]

Would I tweak this text? Absolutely! Skimming it, I see several places where the copy doesn't accurately communicate with the right tone. However, I still saved time because polishing copy is quicker and easier than writing three emails from scratch.

Follow-Up Strategies

Here is ChatGPT's explanation of why follow-up conversations with buyers are effective.

> *A conversation between a salesperson and a buyer is often considered an effective way to persuade the buyer to make a purchase due to several reasons:*
>
> 1. *Personal connection: A conversation allows the salesperson to establish a personal connection with the buyer. By engaging in a dialogue, the salesperson can understand the buyer's needs, preferences, and concerns. This personal connection helps build trust and rapport, which are crucial factors in influencing a buyer's decision.*
> 2. *Active listening: In a conversation, the salesperson can actively listen to the buyer's needs and concerns. By listening attentively, the salesperson can better understand the buyer's motivations and address any objections or doubts. This demonstrates empathy and shows that the salesperson genuinely cares about satisfying the buyer's needs.*
> 3. *Tailored approach: Through a conversation, the salesperson can gather important information about the buyer's specific requirements. This allows the*

salesperson to customize their pitch and present the product or service in a way that directly addresses the buyer's unique needs. Tailoring the sales pitch increases the chances of persuading the buyer by showcasing the value and benefits that are most relevant to them.

4. *Real-time feedback: A conversation enables immediate feedback from the buyer. The salesperson can gauge the buyer's reactions, respond to their questions, and adapt their approach accordingly. This flexibility ensures that the salesperson can address any concerns or objections in real-time, increasing the likelihood of overcoming any barriers to making the purchase.*

5. *Building credibility: By engaging in a conversation, the salesperson has the opportunity to demonstrate their expertise, knowledge, and credibility. They can provide relevant information, answer questions, and share success stories or testimonials. This helps to establish the salesperson as a trusted advisor and positions their product or service as a reliable solution to the buyer's needs.*

6. *Overcoming objections: In a conversation, the salesperson can proactively address any objections or hesitations the buyer may have. They can clarify misconceptions, provide additional information, or offer alternatives to overcome any reservations. This back-and-forth dialogue allows the salesperson to build a persuasive case by directly addressing the buyer's concerns.*

Overall, a conversation allows for a more personalized and interactive experience, facilitating effective communication and understanding between the salesperson and the buyer. By leveraging active listening, tailoring their approach, and addressing objections, a salesperson can build trust, demonstrate value, and ultimately persuade the buyer to make a purchase.

Like much of the information from ChatGPT, there are no big surprises for sales pros, but it serves as a helpful reminder of what you already know.

When a buyer feels a sense of urgency and is ready to buy, they may be eager to move forward. It is easy to spot a situation like this because the buyer will be direct, asking questions such as:

- How quickly can you get me a price?
- When can I see a demo?
- Can I get a sample this week?

In other scenarios, the buyer is interested, but their need is not critical, and they are juggling other priorities and tasks. When this happens, you need a follow-up strategy that builds a relationship, provides value, and earns another meeting.

Your strategy must:

- Create top-of-mind awareness so buyers remember to reach out when they are ready to take the next step in their buying journey.
- Strengthen your relationship after the initial meeting, even when you are not physically present.
- Educate buyers on your value proposition so they understand why it is in their best interests to consider a purchase.

Here are types of touches commonly used by sales pros in follow-up strategies:

- Voice messages and texts containing something of interest.
- Emails directing buyers to relevant information about their company, including blog posts or videos.
- Company brochures sent in PDFs or mailed to buyers.
- Case studies and white papers.
- Branded premiums.
- Personal notes mailed or sent through LinkedIn messaging.
- Relevant industry information.
- An invitation to a company event.
- A testimonial from a happy customer.
- In-depth details about something, like implementing a solution.

Remember, buyers get lots and lots of emails. They get very few pieces of mail, compelling text messages, or worthwhile LinkedIn messages.

When you only send emails, it's a one-note song. If your emails do nothing beyond continually asking for something, you risk annoying busy buyers, even when they are interested.

Look for ways to mix up your touches. Call, text, or send a LinkedIn message to prospects. Mail something. Variety sets you apart from competitors and makes buying from you more interesting for your lead, and ChatGPT can help you create messages for all types of touches.

In the previous chapter, we discussed using ChatGPT to create 'meeting bait,' like executive summaries, case studies, presentations, and sell sheets. These content items also work well as part of your follow-up strategy.

When you mail information with a business letter, you add an element of professionalism. Letters also provide a vehicle for directing the buyer's attention to key points supported by the enclosed information.

AI Letter-Writing

Three-paragraph business letters are long enough to cover everything you need to say and short enough to keep a buyer's attention. ChatGPT can function as your virtual letter-writing assistant and save you time.

The **first paragraph** combines pleasantries with an introduction. It explains why you are sending the buyer information.

The **second paragraph** makes essential points. It could mention specific benefits, demonstrate a competitive advantage, or address a concern often raised by buyers. Bullets work well within this paragraph because they help important points stand out when buyers skim information. If you have a testimonial from a happy customer, you could also ask ChatGPT to include it as part of the second paragraph.

The **third paragraph** wraps everything up and includes a call to action.

By following a few basic prompt tips, anyone can write a sales letter.

Paragraph	Prompt Tips
One	<ul><li>Tell ChatGPT you want to write a friendly and professional letter with no more than 300 words.</li><li>Define the audience and the goal you want your letter to achieve.</li><li>Provide guidelines for the introductory paragraph, including what you are sending and why you think it will help the buyer.</li></ul>

Two	• Outline the key points that benefit the buyer. • If you want the points to be presented in a bulleted list, specify you want an introductory sentence supported by three to five bullets.
Three	• State a conclusion based on the information you have provided. • Include a call-to-action requesting the buyer take the next step.

Let's look at an example.

Imagine a salesperson met with a buyer. A week after the meeting, the marketing team at the salesperson's company released a new brochure. The salesperson decided to send it to the buyer with a letter.

Based on that, I input this prompt into ChatGPT: ***Write a three-paragraph business letter of no more than 300 words using a friendly, professional tone. The audience is a buyer. Their title is purchasing director. The purpose of this letter is to provide more information about my company and get another meeting with the buyer. I will enclose my company's new overview brochure to provide more information. The brochure discusses how we fulfill custom orders within four days compared to the industry standard of ten days. The brochure also talks about our rigorous quality program and friendly customer service.***

The three paragraphs in the letter are structured as follows:

- *Paragraph one includes a friendly opener and explains why I am sending the brochure.*
- *Paragraph two has an opening sentence and lists the benefits as bullets. The benefits are delivering custom orders in 4 days while the industry standard is 10 days, a rigorous quality program, and excellent customer service.*
- *Paragraph three states that I hope the buyer found value in the information. It includes a call to action asking the buyer to meet and discuss how my company's custom order program would benefit them.*

Here is the first result:

Dear [Buyer's Name],

I hope this letter finds you well. I wanted to take a moment to express my gratitude for the opportunity to meet with you and discuss our company, [Your Company Name]. Following our conversation, I am enclosing our new overview brochure, which provides detailed information about our products and services. I believe this brochure will give you a better understanding of how we can be a valuable partner for your company.

In the brochure, you will find that our custom order fulfillment time is significantly faster than the industry standard. We take pride in delivering custom orders within just 4 days, compared to the average 10 days in the market.

Our streamlined processes and efficient supply chain management enable us to offer this quick turnaround time, ensuring that your company can meet tight project deadlines and seize business opportunities promptly. Furthermore, we maintain a rigorous quality program, which guarantees the highest standards in every product we deliver. Our friendly and knowledgeable customer service team is always available to assist you throughout the entire order process, ensuring a smooth and hassle-free experience.

I sincerely hope that you find value in the information provided in our brochure. Our custom order program has proven to be a game-changer for numerous companies in your industry, and I am confident that it would bring significant benefits to [Buyer's Company Name] as well. I would appreciate the opportunity to meet with you again to discuss in further detail how our custom order program can specifically cater to your company's needs. Please let me know a convenient time for us to connect and explore the possibilities.

Thank you for your time and consideration. I look forward to hearing from you soon and continuing our conversation.

Yours sincerely,

I specified bullets in the second paragraph, but the first version of the letter didn't include them, and it had four paragraphs instead of three.

To correct these issues, I wrote another prompt referencing the letter and saying: **Rewrite the information above so the second paragraph is turned into three bullets instead of a**

paragraph of information and combine the third and fourth paragraphs into one ending paragraph.

ChatGPT revised the letter. This time, it had a second paragraph containing bullets.

Dear [Buyer's Name],

I hope this letter finds you well. I wanted to take a moment to express my gratitude for the opportunity to meet with you and discuss our company, [Your Company Name]. Following our conversation, I am enclosing our new overview brochure, which provides detailed information about our products and services. I believe this brochure will give you a better understanding of how we can be a valuable partner for your company.

In the brochure, you will find three key benefits that set us apart from competitors:

- *Custom Order Fulfillment in 4 Days: We pride ourselves on our industry-leading turnaround time. While the average industry standard is 10 days, we deliver custom orders within just 4 days. Our streamlined processes and efficient supply chain management enable us to meet tight project deadlines and seize business opportunities promptly.*
- *Rigorous Quality Program: We maintain a stringent quality program that ensures the highest standards in every product we deliver. From materials sourcing to production and final inspection, we pay meticulous attention to detail, guaranteeing superior quality and customer satisfaction.*

- *Friendly Customer Service: Our dedicated and knowledgeable customer service team is always ready to assist you throughout the entire order process. We strive to provide a smooth and hassle-free experience, offering personalized support and prompt responses to your inquiries.*

I sincerely hope that you find value in the information provided in our brochure. Our custom order program has proven to be a game-changer for numerous companies in your industry, and I am confident that it would bring significant benefits to [Buyer's Company Name] as well. I would appreciate the opportunity to meet with you again to discuss in further detail how our custom order program can specifically cater to your company's needs. Please let me know a convenient time for us to connect and explore the possibilities.

Thank you for your time and consideration. I look forward to hearing from you soon and continuing our conversation.

Yours sincerely,

The second prompt fixed my bullet issue, but I still got a fourth paragraph saying, "Thank you for your time and consideration. I look forward to hearing from you soon and continuing our conversation."

I tried rewriting the prompt again. That line remained and the letter looked a little long to me, so I checked the word count and discovered the second version above contained 321 words in the body copy.

At this point, I could continue tweaking my prompts in ChatGPT or accept what I got and polish it outside the system. My choice would be to accept it and edit it manually using the basic framework.

Are there other ways you can use ChatGPT to develop follow-up strategies? Yes! This book was written as a 'get-started guide,' not an 'all-inclusive compendium.' It's a starting point for your personal exploration of a valuable tool that can help in many ways, including providing ideas for overcoming barriers in the sales process. Let's examine that next.

Chapter Eleven

Overcoming Barriers to a Sale

Every sales pro knows buyers often cling to the status quo, even when the current solution creates problems that the proposed solution solves. When a buyer finally admits they may need something better, it opens the door to change. This creates an opportunity, but you must still bust through any remaining barriers.

Barriers come in a variety of forms, including the following:

- Stated objections: A fully formed thought where the buyer tells you something they don't like about your solution.
- Unstated objections: The buyer doesn't like something, but they keep their thoughts to themselves and don't bring their complaint to light.
- Concerns: The buyer isn't ready to admit your solution is right for them, but they can't verbalize precisely why they feel that way.
- Fears and Aversion to Risk: Buyers worry about the unknown. Doubts can pop up about untried

solutions, the reliability of new vendors, and whether the seller overlooked important information.

- Input from Co-workers: Even when the buyer is the sole decision-maker, they may seek input from their co-workers. Trusted peers can raise barriers by asking questions that buyers can't answer.

ChatGPT can help sales professionals overcome barriers. Let's take an example.

Bucky Overcomes Sales Barriers

Bucky Brown sold corrugated boxes to manufacturers. He scheduled an appointment with a new prospect named Lori Smith. She is the purchasing director at Man-U-Z Company.

Bucky has sold boxes for over a decade, is a top performer, and knows his product. Often, he trades ideas with other members of the sales team. Recently, they talked about using AI, and Bucky decided to use ChatGPT to plan his upcoming call with Lori and see if it could help him close the sale.

He started with this prompt: ***What concerns would a buyer of corrugated boxes at a manufacturing company have about switching box suppliers?***

ChatGPT responded as follows:

When considering a switch in box suppliers, a buyer at a manufacturing company may have several concerns. Here are some common concerns they might have:

1. *Quality: The buyer would be concerned about the quality of the corrugated boxes provided by the new supplier. They would want assurance that the boxes meet the required standards and specifications, as any compromise in quality could lead to damaged products during transit or storage.*

2. *Reliability: Reliability is crucial when it comes to suppliers. The buyer would want to ensure that the new supplier can consistently deliver the required quantity of boxes on time. Any delays or disruptions in the supply chain could adversely affect production schedules and overall operations.*

3. *Cost: Cost is a significant consideration for any manufacturing company. The buyer would want to evaluate the pricing offered by the new supplier and compare it with their existing supplier. They would need to determine if the switch would lead to cost savings or if it would impact their budget negatively.*

4. *Customization and Flexibility: Depending on the specific requirements of the products being packaged, the buyer may need customized corrugated boxes. They would want to assess whether the new supplier can accommodate their customization needs and provide the required flexibility in terms of box sizes, printing options, or special features.*

5. *Supplier's Reputation: The buyer would likely research the new supplier's reputation within the industry. They might check for references or reviews from other companies who have used their services.*

A supplier with a positive reputation for reliability, customer service, and overall performance would instill confidence in the buyer.

6. Environmental Considerations: Sustainability and environmental responsibility are growing concerns for many companies. The buyer may want to ensure that the new supplier follows eco-friendly practices and uses recycled or recyclable materials for their corrugated boxes. They might also look for certifications or accreditations related to sustainable packaging.

7. Transition Process: Switching suppliers involves a transition process, which could include adjustments to logistics, inventory management, and potentially retraining employees on new packaging procedures. The buyer would want to assess how smooth the transition would be and if the new supplier can provide any support or assistance during this phase.

8. Long-Term Partnership: When switching suppliers, the buyer would ideally be seeking a long-term partnership. They would want to assess the new supplier's commitment to customer service, responsiveness to inquiries or issues, and their willingness to collaborate and grow together in the future.

These concerns may vary based on the specific needs and priorities of the manufacturing company, but they provide a good starting point for a buyer considering a switch in box suppliers.

Bucky read the information. While there were no surprises, one point about the transition process made him think. His company did an outstanding job in this area, but Bucky usually didn't discuss the process until the buyer was ready to purchase.

Bucky decided he would bring up the topic of transitioning vendors in the first call and see if the buyer had any concerns to address. He wrote a prompt to collect more information, starting with the information already furnished, followed by a question.

Here is his prompt: **Transition Process: Switching suppliers involves a transition process, which could include adjustments to logistics, inventory management, and potentially retraining employees on new packaging procedures. The buyer would want to assess how smooth the transition would be and if the new supplier can provide any support or assistance during this phase. Based on this information, what exactly would a buyer want to know about transitioning to a new vendor?**

ChatGPT answered.

When transitioning to a new vendor, a buyer would want to gather specific information to assess the smoothness of the transition and understand the support and assistance provided by the new supplier. Here are some key questions a buyer might want to ask:

1. *Transition Timeline: What is the estimated timeline for the transition process from the current supplier to the new vendor? Understanding the duration helps*

the buyer plan for any potential disruptions or adjustments in their operations.

2. *Inventory Management: How will the transition impact inventory management? The buyer would want to know if there will be any changes in inventory levels, lead times, or order placement procedures during the transition. This helps the buyer ensure a smooth flow of materials and avoid any inventory shortages or excesses.*

3. *Logistics and Delivery: How will the new supplier handle logistics and delivery? The buyer would want to understand if there are any changes in shipping methods, carriers, or delivery schedules. This ensures that the products can continue to be delivered on time and in the desired condition.*

4. *Packaging Specifications: Will there be any adjustments to the packaging specifications or requirements? The buyer would want to know if they need to modify their product packaging, labeling, or any other related aspects. This information helps them ensure compliance with industry standards and customer expectations.*

5. *Training and Support: Will the new supplier provide training and support during the transition period? The buyer would want to know if the supplier offers assistance in training their employees on new packaging procedures or any other adjustments required. This helps ensure a seamless integration of the new supplier's products into the manufacturing process.*

6. *Communication Channels: What communication channels will be established between the buyer and the new supplier? The buyer would want to establish effective lines of communication to address any questions, concerns, or issues that may arise during the transition. They might inquire about the availability of dedicated account managers or customer support teams.*

7. *Performance Monitoring: How will the buyer and the new supplier monitor and evaluate the performance of the transition? The buyer would want to know if there will be any performance metrics or key performance indicators (KPIs) established to assess the success of the transition. This helps ensure that any necessary adjustments can be made promptly.*

8. *Contingency Plans: Does the new supplier have contingency plans in place to handle any unexpected challenges or issues during the transition? The buyer would want to assess the supplier's preparedness and ability to respond to potential disruptions, such as delays or quality concerns, during the transition period.*

By gathering this information, the buyer can evaluate how well the new supplier addresses their concerns and provides support throughout the transition process. This helps minimize risks and ensures a smooth switch to the new vendor.

Bucky used the follow-up information to create a 'frequently asked questions' document for Lori, covering possible concerns about transitioning to a new supplier.

To further understand the buyer's point of view, he decided to ask one more pre-call question and input this: **What questions could a buyer of corrugated boxes ask a salesperson in a sales call?**

ChatGPT responded with a substantial list:

During a sales call with a salesperson representing a corrugated box supplier, a buyer may ask the following questions to gather relevant information and make an informed decision:

Product Specifications:

- *What types of corrugated boxes does your company offer?*
- *Can you provide details on the materials used and the durability of your boxes?*
- *What are the available sizes and dimensions?*
- *Are there any customization options available, such as printing, special coatings, or inserts?*

Pricing and Terms:

- *What is the pricing structure for your corrugated boxes?*
- *Are there any volume discounts or long-term contract options?*
- *Do you have a minimum order quantity requirement?*

- What are the payment terms and accepted payment methods?

Production Capacity and Lead Time:

- What is your production capacity for corrugated boxes?
- How quickly can you fulfill orders and deliver the boxes?
- Are there any lead times or production constraints to consider?
- How do you handle rush orders or urgent requests?

Quality Assurance:

- What quality control measures do you have in place to ensure the boxes meet industry standards?
- Do you have any certifications or accreditations related to quality?
- Can you provide samples or references from other customers who have used your boxes?

Sustainability and Environmental Practices:

- What steps does your company take to promote sustainability in corrugated box manufacturing?
- Are your boxes made from recycled or recyclable materials?
- Do you have any eco-friendly certifications or initiatives in place?

Supply Chain and Logistics:

- How do you handle shipping and logistics for delivering the boxes?

- *Can you provide information on the shipping costs and carriers you work with?*
- *Do you have experience working with companies in our industry or with similar packaging requirements?*

Customer Support and Services:

- *What kind of customer support do you offer?*
- *Is there a dedicated account manager or point of contact for inquiries and assistance?*
- *How do you handle customer feedback or any issues that may arise?*
- *Can you provide references or testimonials from current customers?*

Long-Term Partnership:

- *What is your company's approach to building long-term partnerships with customers?*
- *Can you describe any value-added services or additional benefits your company provides?*
- *Are there any plans for future product innovations or improvements?*

These questions help the buyer gather essential information about the supplier's offerings, pricing, quality, sustainability practices, logistics, and customer support. By asking these questions, the buyer can evaluate the compatibility of the supplier with their specific requirements and make an informed decision.

Bucky skimmed the list. His experience told him which questions were likely to come up in a first meeting and which were irrelevant. The list made him consider how he 'sold' the company's customer service team. Even if Lori didn't ask any of the four questions about customer service, Bucky knew she would still weigh those factors when deciding whether to change vendors. He decided to be proactive and bring up customer service during his first call, answering the questions before they were asked and offering to provide references.

Bucky's first call with Lori went fantastically well! She told him she was interested in getting pricing. First, she needed to check the current inventory levels and discuss changing vendors with Rhonda Jenner, the Vice President of Operations and Lori's boss.

A strong follow-up strategy at this stage was critical. Bucky was confident Lori was the decision-maker. Even though the meeting went well, he knew obstacles could still derail the sale. He decided to ask ChatGPT about possible objections using this prompt: **What are all the objections a buyer could raise when selecting a new corrugated box supplier?**

ChatGPT responded with this answer.

> *When selecting a new corrugated box supplier, a buyer may raise various objections or concerns. These objections can vary depending on the specific needs and priorities of the buyer and their organization. Here are some common objections that a buyer could raise:*
>
> *Quality Concerns:*

- *"How can I be sure that the boxes provided by the new supplier will meet our quality standards?"*
- *"What quality control measures do you have in place to ensure consistent box quality?"*
- *"Do you have any certifications or accreditations related to box quality?"*

Reliability and Delivery:

- *"Can you guarantee on-time delivery and consistent supply of boxes?"*
- *"How do you handle unexpected disruptions or delays in the supply chain?"*
- *"What is your track record for meeting delivery schedules?"*

Cost and Pricing:

- *"How does your pricing compare to our current supplier or other competitors?"*
- *"Can you provide a breakdown of the costs associated with the corrugated boxes?"*
- *"Are there any hidden or additional charges that we should be aware of?"*

Customization and Flexibility:

- *"Can you accommodate our specific customization needs, such as printing, sizing, or special features?"*
- *"How flexible are you in terms of adjusting box specifications if our requirements change?"*
- *"What is the lead time for customized or special order boxes?"*

Supplier's Capabilities:

- *"Do you have the capacity to handle our volume requirements?"*
- *"What other customers do you currently serve in our industry?"*
- *"Can you provide references or testimonials from your existing customers?"*

Environmental Considerations:

- *"What sustainable practices do you have in place for corrugated box production?"*
- *"Are your boxes made from recycled or recyclable materials?"*
- *"Can you provide documentation or evidence of your environmental commitments?"*

Transition and Support:

- *"What is your process for transitioning from our current supplier to your company?"*
- *"Can you provide assistance or support during the transition phase?"*
- *"How do you handle any potential disruptions during the switch to your supplier?"*

Long-Term Partnership:

- *"What is your approach to building long-term partnerships with customers?"*
- *"How do you handle customer feedback or address issues that may arise?"*

> - *"What additional value-added services or benefits do you offer?"*
>
> *By raising these objections and concerns, the buyer can gather more information, address potential risks, and evaluate the suitability of the new corrugated box supplier for their specific requirements.*

Bucky reviewed the objections and his notes from the sales call. While he believed Lori was interested in buying, he didn't sense any urgency about making an immediate change. That indicated he needed a long-haul follow-up strategy. He decided to use ChatGPT to write one email a week. He chose to start by discussing capacity because it was a concern Lori raised during their meeting. Though he had mentioned his company ran two shifts, Lori hadn't taken many notes, so he decided to mention it in his first email. His prompt said: **Write a 100-word email using a friendly, professional tone as a follow-up to a sales meeting with a corrugated box buyer. Tell the buyer my company runs two shifts and has plenty of capacity to meet their volume requirements. Include an invitation to visit our manufacturing plant to see our operations.**

ChatGPT came back with this:

> *Dear [Buyer's Name],*
>
> *I hope this email finds you well. It was a pleasure meeting you during our recent sales meeting.*

> *I wanted to follow up and reiterate my company's commitment to meeting your corrugated box needs.*
>
> *I wanted to emphasize that our manufacturing plant runs two shifts, enabling us to maximize our production capacity. Rest assured, we have more than enough capacity to meet your volume requirements effectively and efficiently.*
>
> *To provide you with a deeper understanding of our operations, I extend an invitation for you to visit our manufacturing plant. It would be a great opportunity for you to witness firsthand how we maintain high-quality standards while fulfilling large orders. Please let me know a convenient time, and we will gladly arrange a tour for you.*
>
> *Thank you for considering our services, and we look forward to the possibility of working together. Should you have any further questions or require additional information, please don't hesitate to reach out.*
>
> *Warm regards,*

Bucky liked the basic structure, but the wording was a little clunky. He tweaked it and sent it to Lori. A week passed, and she didn't respond, so he chose a different objection and created another email.

Every week for the next six weeks, Bucky sent an email. Along with capacity, his topics addressed quality, on-time delivery, service, and product customization. He also called, sent Lori an invitation to link on LinkedIn, and mailed her a new company brochure about eco-friendly packaging along with a letter written with help from ChatGPT.

At the end of the sixth week, Bucky finally got a call from Lori.

"Thanks for keeping in touch," she said. "Our current supplier missed a couple of critical delivery dates, and it caused a lot of problems. I went to my boss and said we needed to change. It came down to you and one other company." Lori chuckled, "But really, it wasn't much of a contest. Those emails you sent—it was like you were reading my mind! You addressed all my concerns without me bringing them up. Can you come by next Tuesday and talk about the next steps?"

What can we learn from Bucky and his experience with ChatGPT?

While ChatGPT can save time, Bucky's primary motivation for trying out the system was gathering fresh ideas to improve closing sales. Using ChatGPT helped Bucky with pre-call planning and his follow-up strategy.

Bucky's initial prompts helped him gather intelligence on the factors a buyer could consider when evaluating new vendors and questions that might be asked. It was good information, especially when combined with Bucky's selling expertise, and it helped him better anticipate and overcome barriers. He also used the information to develop a FAQ sheet for Lori that answered common questions buyers often had about transitioning between vendors.

The call went well, but the deal didn't close immediately. Bucky turned to ChatGPT to help craft follow-up emails. The topics reflected Lori's concerns in their conversation and other potential objections. For the next six weeks, he sent one email a week to Lori using ChatGPT for assistance. He also called, reached out through LinkedIn, and mailed her a company brochure.

After sending the sixth email, Bucky heard from Lori. She was finally ready to proceed with an order, and Bucky closed the sale.

Bucky used ChatGPT to anticipate and eliminate potential barriers to closing. The system helped him craft a series of well-constructed follow-up emails. While it required time, Bucky's investment paid off when he closed the sale.

Besides creating information Bucky could repurpose and reuse to overcome barriers, objections, and concerns and close future deals, the exercise helped a sales pro sharpen his skills.

Are there other ways that ChatGPT can be used as a sales training tool?

Yes, there are! Let's explore a few options.

Chapter Twelve

Self-Coaching Using ChatGPT

In sales, you can't always win, but you will win more often if you can outsell the competition because you have better skills.

ChatGPT can serve as your virtual coach, providing personalized information to help you improve in any area where you choose to focus, including:

- Relationship building.
- Product knowledge and presenting benefits to potential buyers.
- Selling skills such as getting meetings, getting opportunities, overcoming objections, and closing deals.
- Account management.
- Communicating your company's value proposition and differentiators.

This chapter will take a generalized approach to learning, which you can apply to any area, starting with a few basics on how we all learn.

The Science of Learning

When you are exposed to new information about selling, you learn when you relate the latest information to what you already know. Retention-worthy information is stored in your long-term memory. Memories must be retrieved before information can be used in upskilling activities.

Repeated exposure deepens connections to memories, making them easier to retrieve. It's common for this type of learning strategy to be found in elementary schools, where teachers teach basics like multiplication and spelling with repetition drills.

Once fundamentals are learned and relevant content is easy to access in our memory, we build on this by focusing on the meaning of the content and better ways of applying it. Putting new knowledge to use in sales situations provides immediate feedback. Combining feedback with critical thinking shows you how to use the knowledge to finetune your selling skills.

ChatGPT can help expand background knowledge by answering questions, offering context, and explaining concepts. You can use it to generate examples and develop scenarios for selling situations. The system can provide ideas and strategies for approaching tasks and everyday occurrences, and by using it to add new layers of knowledge to skillsets, you can gain a competitive advantage in your market.

Let's start with one of the fastest and easiest ways to use ChatGPT for skill-building: retrieving information you already know and finding new ways to use it.

Access and Recall Information

Has this ever happened to you? You make a sales call, the potential buyer asks a question, and you bungle the answer.

The call ends, and you head to your car. As you step onto the pavement in the parking lot, you think of a BRILLIANT answer to the question asked by the buyer. Frustration seeps through you as you wonder why you couldn't grab the knowledge when it was needed.

Sales conversations are rapid-fire interactions. There isn't a lot of deep, introspective thinking going on, either by you or the buyer. Ammunition comes from easily remembered knowledge.

ChatGPT prompts can call up information you know but seldom use. Reactivating knowledge before you are in a selling situation creates opportunities to use it and improve call outcomes.

Using ChatGPT to access information buried deep in your brain works like this:

- Ask ChatGPT a question relevant to an upcoming call.
- Review the answer.

- Refine your prompt if necessary.
- Print the answer.
- Review it at least three times before making the call.

Pulling knowledge out of mental storage and dusting it off gives you more options when you respond to buyers.

The following are a few examples of effective prompts for gathering general information using this self-learning method:

- What benefits do buyers who purchase <product/service> for the <buyer's industry> want from a vendor?
- What concerns would a buyer who purchases <product/service> for a <buyer's industry> have about changing vendors?
- What questions could a buyer who purchases <product/service> for a <buyer's industry> ask a sales representative?
- What objections could a buyer who purchases <product/service> in the <buyer's industry> raise because they had concerns about changing vendors?

You can also use this method to focus on something specific, using a prompt like, ***"If a buyer says, 'Your price is higher than my current vendor,' how could a sales representative respond to that objection?"***

These types of prompts provide broad-based information for a general review. Let's examine another smart way to use ChatGPT to improve outcomes.

Scenarios and Examples

Scenarios are hypothetical situations that could occur. They describe a sequence of events or circumstances or a theoretical interaction between people in different roles, like a buyer and a sales pro. An example is a specific instance that illustrates a concept and clarifies an explanation.

I input this prompt into ChatGPT to get AI's insight on the topic: **How can visualizing scenarios and situational examples help salespeople improve their selling skills?**

Here is ChatGPT's response:

Visualizing scenarios and situational examples can greatly aid salespeople in enhancing their selling skills in a number of ways. Here are some of the main reasons:

1. *Improve Communication Skills: By visualizing scenarios, salespeople can work on their communication and interpersonal skills. It provides them an opportunity to practice and refine their pitch, and work on their tone, language, and non-verbal communication.*

2. *Customer Understanding: Visualization can help salespeople get into the shoes of their customers. By doing so, they gain a better understanding of the customer's needs, preferences, and potential objections. This can help them tailor their approach to each individual customer.*

3. *Enhances Confidence: Visualization of successful sales scenarios can help to build confidence. By*

seeing themselves succeed in their mind's eye, salespeople can overcome anxiety and approach each sales encounter with more poise and assurance.

4. *Preparation for Different Scenarios: Not all sales interactions follow the same script. Visualization can prepare salespeople for a variety of potential situations. They can mentally rehearse how they would handle difficult customers, objections, or unexpected questions.*

5. *Solution Selling: By visualizing different scenarios, salespeople can practice illustrating how their product or service can solve the customer's problem. They can envision how to demonstrate the value proposition in a compelling manner that aligns with the customer's needs.*

6. *Closing Skills: Visualization can also help in practicing closing techniques. By imagining different scenarios, salespeople can perfect their timing, technique, and responses to ensure they close the deal effectively.*

7. *Empathy and Connection: By visualizing from the customer's perspective, salespeople can develop empathy. This helps build a connection with the customer, which is crucial for trust and long-term relationship building.*

Remember, like any other skill, the benefits of visualization are gained through regular and sustained practice. The more a salesperson practices visualizing scenarios, the better they will become at handling real-life sales situations.

To develop a helpful learning scenario, you must include enough context to make a situation come to life. The following are tips for building an effective prompt:

- Define what you want. "Describe a scenario where . . ." works well as a starting point.
- Provide a bulleted list of factors affecting the situation.
- State the outcome.
- State the delivery format for the information. Do you want it to mimic a conversation or read like a story?

Here is an illustration of how this could work for a salesperson who sells folding cartons and is trying to break into a cereal manufacturing company. The rep wants to prepare to respond to a pricing objection.

Building Your Prompt	Example
Define what you want.	Describe a scenario where a sales representative is trying to get the first order from a new buyer and must deal with the following circumstances.
State factors affecting the situation.	<ul><li>It would be the buyer's first time making a purchase.</li><li>The buyer had the salesperson quote a box</li></ul>

	for an upcoming order before the meeting.
	• The buyer reviews the price and tells the sales representative their price is higher than the current vendor's.
	• In a past meeting, the buyer mentioned quality issues with the current vendor.
	• The buyer also says they are impressed with the buyer's quality and would like to do business.
Outcome	The salesperson responds to the price objection positively and, after further discussion, gets the order.
Format	Return the scenario in a story format.

Here is the scenario ChatGPT provided:

With a bit of anticipation and a well-prepared plan, Sales Representative Sarah arrived at the company. It was the first time she was going to secure an order from this potential buyer. She could sense the opportunities it could bring, and she was determined to make it count.

A few days before, the potential buyer had requested a quote from Sarah for a box that they were looking to order. As they sat across the table in the modern conference room, the buyer reviewed Sarah's quote. He leaned back and looked at Sarah, "I have to tell you, Sarah, your price is higher than our current vendor's."

Sarah knew that price was always a sensitive topic, and she anticipated such a challenge. However, she also remembered a previous meeting where the buyer mentioned dissatisfaction with the current vendor due to quality issues.

Taking a calm breath, Sarah responded, "I appreciate your transparency, and I understand that the price might be a concern. However, I believe we should also consider the overall value that our product brings. In our past meeting, you shared some quality issues with your current vendor. We pride ourselves on the top-notch quality of our products, and it's clear you've noticed the difference."

Sarah paused for a moment to let her words sink in. "When you factor in the potential cost of dealing with quality issues – in terms of both time and money – our price can be very competitive. Also, it's our aim to establish a long-term relationship with our clients, ensuring a reliable, high-quality supply for your needs."

The buyer nodded, seemingly appreciative of her points. Sarah noticed a glimmer of interest in the buyer's eyes and continued, "Furthermore, we value your business and want to ensure you receive the best value for your money. While we are confident in our product's superior quality, we are

> open to discussing flexible pricing options, especially as our business relationship grows."
>
> The buyer looked thoughtfully at Sarah. He liked her approach, her professionalism, and, most importantly, her understanding of his needs. After further discussion around their potential collaboration, he smiled and extended his hand across the table.
>
> "Sarah, I'm convinced. I appreciate your commitment to quality and customer service, and I'm eager to start doing business with you. Let's go ahead with this order."
>
> As Sarah shook his hand, she felt a sense of achievement. Her preparation and strategic approach had paid off, opening a new door for their business partnership.

If you prefer, your scenario format can shift from a story to a conversation by changing the last line of the prompt to **"Return the scenario in a format mimicking a conversation."**

ChatGPT responded with this:

> Salesperson (S): Hello, thank you for taking the time to meet with me today. I understand you have our quote for the upcoming order.
>
> Buyer (B): Yes, I have it right here. I have to say, I've reviewed your price, and it's higher than what our current vendor is offering.
>
> S: I understand your concern. Price is certainly a crucial factor in making such decisions. However, if I may recall,

during our last meeting, you had mentioned some quality issues with your current vendor, is that correct?

B: Yes, that's true. We've had a few issues with their product's quality lately.

S: I think that's an important point to consider. While we might not be the cheapest option upfront, our consistent high-quality products could lead to fewer issues down the line, potentially saving you both time and money in terms of reduced wastage and fewer returns. I believe it was the quality of our product that you were impressed with initially, right?

B: Yes, I have to admit, the quality of your product has caught our eye. We would like to do business, but the price difference is a significant factor for us.

S: Absolutely, I understand where you're coming from. However, it's important to view the cost from a broader perspective, beyond the initial purchase. By investing in higher quality, you could also be boosting your own customer satisfaction and brand reputation. Not to mention, potential cost savings from not having to deal with defective products or returns.

B: You make a good point. I guess it's a matter of considering the bigger picture.

S: Precisely. With our commitment to quality, I can assure you that we will be a reliable partner for you. We're not just selling a product, but we're offering peace of mind and reliability. And we're willing to support you to make this

> *transition as smooth as possible. Shall we proceed with this order?*
>
> *B: I appreciate your understanding and the insights you've shared. I think you're right, we need to look at the long-term benefits. Let's proceed with the order.*

Creating scenarios helps you anticipate possible hurdles and how you can overcome them.

Examples are a little more straightforward. Start your prompt with the phrase, "Give me an example," followed by other details.

Sticking with the pricing theme, let's look at an example using this prompt: **Give me an example of how a salesperson could respond to a buyer who tells them their price is too high.**

ChatGPT responded:

> *Sure, here's an example of how a salesperson might respond to a buyer who states that the price is too high:*
>
> ***Buyer (B):*** *Your price is too high compared to what we've seen elsewhere.*
>
> ***Salesperson (S):*** *I understand where you're coming from, and price is certainly an important factor when making a purchasing decision. May I ask, what are some of the key criteria you're considering for this purchase beyond just the price?*

B: Well, we're looking for reliability, quality, and a good customer support service.

S: Those are certainly crucial factors. While our price might initially seem higher, we excel in all the areas you've just mentioned.

Our product is known for its reliability, which means you won't face unexpected downtime or the need for frequent replacements. This could actually save you money in the long run.

When it comes to quality, our product has been recognized as industry-leading, ensuring that it not only lasts longer but performs better. This can help enhance your productivity and prevent potential losses from defects or failures.

Lastly, our customer service is top-notch. We're here to support you 24/7, ensuring any questions or issues you may have are addressed promptly and effectively. This level of service can save you a significant amount of time and prevent potential headaches.

In essence, while we might not be the cheapest option upfront, our total value proposition is designed to save you money and provide peace of mind over the long term. Would you consider these factors when assessing the overall cost and benefits of our offering?

This prompt asked a general question. It didn't include any context about the product or service sold or the buyer's industry. Therefore, the response was also generalized and non-specific.

Using ChatGPT to construct scenarios or examples helps you anticipate selling situations and plan a response. When a situation doesn't go as you hoped, it can also help you recognize where a call went off track.

Diagnosing to Improve

We asked ChatGPT this question: ***How can a salesperson use ChatGPT to diagnose what may have gone wrong in a sales call?***

ChatGPT responded:

Using AI like ChatGPT to diagnose what may have gone wrong in a sales call can be quite useful, especially if you have a recorded transcript of the conversation. Here's how it could work:

1. *Transcript Analysis: If the sales call was recorded and transcribed, a salesperson can input the transcript into ChatGPT, asking it to identify potential missteps. ChatGPT can analyze the conversation for instances of potentially negative language, missed opportunities to empathize with a client's needs, or inadequate responses to objections.*
2. *Sentiment Analysis: ChatGPT can be used to perform sentiment analysis on the sales call transcript. Sentiment analysis allows for the identification of emotional states from the text. For instance, you can identify moments of confusion, irritation, or disinterest from the client, which might indicate problematic areas.*

3. *Coaching and Training: Based on the points of weakness identified, a salesperson can use ChatGPT for role-playing exercises to practice better responses and strategies for similar situations in the future. For example, if ChatGPT identifies that the salesperson struggled to overcome client objections, the salesperson could practice responses to these objections using the AI model.*

4. *Question Generation: ChatGPT can help generate probing questions that the salesperson may have missed during the call. The use of good questions is a fundamental skill for salespeople, helping to uncover needs, build relationships, and close deals. By analyzing the transcript, the AI can suggest questions that could have led to a more productive discussion.*

5. *Review Product Knowledge: If a lack of product knowledge was identified as a problem area, a salesperson could use ChatGPT to brush up on product details and how to communicate these to potential clients effectively.*

It's important to note that while AI can help with these tasks, it's still crucial for the salesperson to exercise their judgment and use their understanding of the situation to interpret the AI's suggestions. Sales is a highly interpersonal field, and it involves a level of nuance and human understanding that AI isn't fully capable of grasping as of my knowledge cut-off in September 2021.

If you record a sales call or online meeting and can produce a transcript, there is real value in asking ChatGPT to analyze the call and provide feedback on how it could have been improved. Recording a conversation is subject to privacy laws, so be sure you follow all legal requirements in your state.

If you don't have a meeting transcript, you could describe what happened in a sales call and ask for feedback. Diagnostic insight is beneficial when a situation fits the following parameters:

- You have a clear recollection of events.
- The buyer was interested in your solution.
- The buyer raised an objection, asked a question, or questioned a benefit.
- You responded.
- The buyer didn't like the response and lost interest.

Outlining a situation like this and asking ChatGPT to diagnose opportunities for improvement provides valuable feedback for future sales calls.

ChatGPT can also be used for diagnosing ways to improve voicemail messages, social communications, business letters, and email messages. Below is an example based on a sales solicitation email sent to my company by an accounting firm.

The original email contained this copy:

Wondering if Thought Transformation could use some help with the books in addition to further accounting tasks.

Would you like to check into easily/cost-effectively keeping your books, allowing you to spend time on what you love doing most?

All you need to do is respond with a good direct number, and we'll be in touch shortly.

I used this information to construct the following prompt:

This is copy from an email selling accounting services:

Wondering if Thought Transformation could use some help with the books, in addition to further accounting tasks.

Would you like to check into easily/cost effectively keep your books, allowing you to spend time on what you love doing most?

All you need to do is respond with a good direct number and we'll be in touch shortly.

How could the email be improved to motivate a buyer to meet with the accounting services firm?

ChatGPT responded:

> *The sales email you provided has a clear goal and a call-to-action, but it could use some more specific details and emotional appeals to increase its persuasiveness. Here's a revised version:*
>
> *Subject: Streamline Thought Transformation's Finances with our Comprehensive Accounting Services*
>
> *Hello [Recipient's Name],*

I hope this message finds you well. As an innovator and leader in your field, you know that your time is best spent focusing on the core activities that drive Thought Transformation forward, rather than the details of balancing the books.

We at [Your Accounting Firm's Name] understand this perfectly. That's why we specialize in providing comprehensive, easy-to-use, and cost-effective accounting services, tailored specifically for businesses like yours.

Our services not only ensure accuracy in your financial reporting, but they also give you more time and peace of mind to invest in what you truly love - innovating and growing your business.

We would love to show you how we can take the burden of accounting off your shoulders and help you focus more on your business growth. Could we schedule a brief, no-obligation consultation at a time that's convenient for you? This would give us a chance to understand your unique needs and demonstrate how our services could add value to Thought Transformation.

Please respond with a suitable date and time, along with your contact number, and we'll be in touch shortly.

We look forward to the opportunity of assisting you in your financial journey.

Best Regards,

[Your Name] [Your Position] [Your Accounting Firm's Name] [Your Contact Details]

> *This version of the email has a few improvements:*
>
> - *Personalization: Using the recipient's name and mentioning their business name makes the email feel more personal and less like a mass marketing message.*
> - *Emphasis on Benefits: Rather than simply stating what the firm does, the email puts the focus on the benefits that the recipient will gain.*
> - *Adding Value: The email offers a no-obligation consultation, which gives the impression that the firm is interested in providing value to the potential client.*
> - *Clear Call to Action: The call to action at the end is clear, yet not too demanding. It gives the recipient an easy way to move forward.*

ChatGPT started by noting the original email could be improved by including more specific details and an emotional appeal. It's a valid diagnosis, and the email generated by the system fixes these problems.

ChatGPT gives you the ability to analyze sales interactions and identify improvement opportunities. You can use it in pre-call planning and post-call analysis to gain insight.

While it is natural to seek feedback when situations don't go well, ChatGPT can also be used to diagnose why a selling situation had a happy conclusion. Knowing why you reached a positive outcome in a situation can motivate you to continue developing your skills and achieve mastery.

Selling Tips

ChatGPT is an excellent tool for creating lists of tips. Let's work through an example focused on trial close questions helpful in gauging whether a buyer is ready to purchase.

The prompt was: **Give me twenty tips for using 'trial close' questions in a sales call.**

ChatGPT responded:

Absolutely, here are twenty tips on using a 'trial close' question effectively in a sales call:

1. *Know your audience: Tailor your trial close question to your prospect's specific needs, pain points, and business objectives.*
2. *Don't rush: Ensure you've provided sufficient information about your product or service before attempting a trial close.*
3. *Listen carefully: Pay attention to the prospect's responses. They can reveal their level of interest and any objections they might have.*
4. *Ask open-ended questions: These types of questions promote discussion and provide more insight than simple yes or no answers.*
5. *Balance confidence with empathy: While it's important to be confident in your offering, also show understanding and concern for your prospect's needs.*
6. *Use trial closes regularly: Don't just use them at the end of the call. They can help guide the conversation and keep you on track.*

7. *Mirror the prospect's language: This can help establish rapport and make your prospect feel understood.*

8. *Practice Active Listening: This not only shows respect but also allows you to gather important information about your prospect's needs and objections.*

9. *Be patient: Allow the prospect sufficient time to think and respond to your trial close question.*

10. *Avoid being pushy: The goal of a trial close is to gauge interest, not to pressure a prospect into buying.*

11. *Be clear and concise: Your question should be easy to understand and straight to the point.*

12. *Don't argue with objections: If a prospect raises objections, treat it as an opportunity to understand their concerns better.*

13. *Prepare for different responses: Have a strategy ready for any possible response, be it positive, negative, or neutral.*

14. *Keep it conversational: Make the trial close feel like a natural part of the conversation.*

15. *Show genuine interest: The trial close should feel less like a sales tactic and more like genuine interest in solving the prospect's problems.*

16. *Follow up: If a prospect seems interested but doesn't immediately commit, ensure to follow up promptly and professionally.*

17. *Use positive language: Frame your trial close in a way that emphasizes the benefits your solution offers.*

18. *Show flexibility: Be ready to adapt your product/service presentation based on the feedback received from the trial close.*

19. *Leverage the power of silence: After asking the trial close question, let the prospect fill the silence. This can often lead to them revealing additional information or objections.*

20. *Continuous Improvement: Always look to refine and improve your trial close questions based on the responses you receive and the outcomes of your sales calls. Use every interaction as a learning opportunity.*

You can print this document or drop the information into a spreadsheet and use it to create flashcards.

If you want to print flashcards, use printable index cards, which are available from online office supply vendors. Printing flashcards is like printing labels for multiple addresses. I use Microsoft Word, which has a wizard built into the program for projects like this. If you are also a Word user, click the 'Mailings' tab and select 'Start Mail Merge' for step-by-step instructions to walk you through the process. ChatGPT can also provide detailed instructions on creating flashcards within other word-processing programs.

Last Thoughts

You can't always win in sales, but you can stack the deck in your favor by honing your skills. That's where AI can help. ChatGPT is your always-on-call, 24/7 virtual sales coach.

When you have a question, grab your phone, and access the system.

ChatGPT is a memory bank and a personalized content library filled with scenarios, examples, and tips. It is a mentor helping you understand what you did right and wrong in all types of selling situations. Sales pros who master ChatGPT and apply the lessons learned through technology aren't just upping their sales game; they are also rewriting the rules.

Let's keep going and find another way to transform learning into progress in another selling skill set.

Chapter Thirteen

Cross-Selling to Win

Cross-selling is one of the smartest ways to grow your book of business because you can increase revenues without acquiring new customers. Success comes from identifying opportunities to sell products or services related to a current purchase and convincing customers to switch and start buying from you.

To start planning your strategy, begin with a prompt built to include the following information:

- State the product or service currently sold to a customer.
- State reasons why the customer chooses to buy it from you.
- State what you want to cross-sell.
- Ask ChatGPT why it would be logical for the customer to buy the additional product from you.

Let's examine Sharon's situation as an example of how AI can help sales pros develop cross-selling strategies.

Sharon sold for a large printing company. A year ago, she opened an account with a furniture company. The buyer, Peter, is the marketing director. He has purchased four brochures and one catalog from Sharon. Several projects had critical deadlines because they were distributed at tradeshows.

Along with marketing collateral, Peter buys tradeshow displays, which Sharon's printing company also produces. She mentioned these additional capabilities to Peter, but he is busy, and she didn't think he gave the topic much thought. Sharon decided to use AI to help her craft a cross-selling strategy.

She started with this prompt: *I sell printed marketing collateral to a customer. The customer works with me because we provide consistently high quality, reliably meet delivery dates, provide consultation to assure the best outcomes, offer value-added suggestions, and are easy to work with. The customer also buys tradeshow displays, which my company also sells. Why would it make sense for the customer to purchase tradeshow displays from my company?*

ChatGPT responded:

> *Given the background information provided, there are several compelling reasons why the customer would benefit from purchasing tradeshow displays from your company:*
>
> *1. Consistent High Quality: Your customer already trusts the quality of your printed marketing collateral. It's logical to*

assume that the same standards of excellence would be applied to your tradeshow displays.

2. Reliability: If your company consistently meets delivery dates for one product line, it's likely you would extend that reliability to other products. This assurance is invaluable, especially when planning for time-sensitive events like tradeshows.

3. Consultation Expertise: Tradeshows are significant investments for companies. The consultation you provide to assure the best outcomes for printed collateral can be even more critical for tradeshow displays, which play a substantial role in a company's public image and branding during the event.

4. Value-added Suggestions: If you already provide value-added suggestions for printed collateral, it's clear you're invested in your customer's success. These insights would be crucial for tradeshow displays, ensuring the customer maximizes their booth's effectiveness and stands out in a crowded event space.

5. Ease of Working Relationship: Developing a strong, easy working relationship takes time. If your customer already enjoys this relationship with you, transitioning to another vendor for tradeshow displays could mean starting from scratch, introducing unnecessary risks and potential inefficiencies.

6. Consistency in Branding: Using the same provider for both printed collateral and tradeshow displays ensures a uniform look and feel. This consistency is key for branding, ensuring that all materials, from brochures to large displays, convey the same message and aesthetic.

7. One-Stop Shop: By sourcing both products from your company, the customer reduces the number of vendors they have to deal with. This can simplify their procurement process, streamline communications, and possibly lead to bundled discounts.

8. Cost Efficiency: Often, working with a single vendor for multiple needs allows for bundled services or volume discounts. Even if the price isn't significantly lower, the value derived from a trusted relationship, coupled with the savings in time and administrative costs, can be substantial.

9. Integrated Design and Strategy: Your knowledge of the customer's marketing collateral can be leveraged to create tradeshow displays that are coherent and integrated with their other marketing efforts.

10. Reduced Risk: Every new vendor a company works with introduces an element of risk. By sticking with a known and trusted entity, the customer reduces the chances of potential issues related to quality, delivery, and communication.

Given these points, it makes significant sense for the customer to consider purchasing tradeshow displays from your company, leveraging the trust, reliability, and value they've already experienced with your printed marketing collateral.

While this information was useful, Sharon wanted to see how ChatGPT would transform it into an actionable plan to help her make the sale.

She followed up her initial query with this prompt: **Based on the information, provide a step-by-step plan to get a meeting to present this information to the client within the next 30 days.**

ChatGPT responded:

Certainly! Here's a step-by-step plan to secure a meeting and present this information to your client within the next 30 days:

1. Research and Preparation:

> *1.1: Review past interactions: Understand the client's past needs, preferences, and pain points.*

> *1.2: Develop a tailored proposal: Highlight the benefits mentioned above, but make sure they are personalized to your client's specific situation.*

> *1.3: Gather evidence: Have case studies, testimonials, or examples of tradeshow displays you've provided to other clients to showcase your capabilities.*

2. Reach Out:

> *2.1: Choose the right medium: If the client prefers email communication, start there. If they value phone calls, then give them a ring.*

2.2: Open with value: Start by expressing appreciation for their trust in your current services and then state your intention to offer them even more value.

2.3: Propose a few potential dates: Give options but ensure they fall within the 30-day window.

3. Follow-Up:

3.1: If there's no response within a week, send a gentle follow-up reminding them of your initial outreach.

3.2: Offer additional flexibility for the meeting time if the proposed slots don't work for them.

4. Prepare the Presentation:

4.1: Create a concise presentation focusing on the benefits of them purchasing tradeshow displays from you.

4.2: Ensure the content is tailored to their brand and needs.

4.3: Prepare answers to potential questions or objections they might have.

5. Confirm the Meeting:

5.1: A few days before the scheduled meeting, send a confirmation email or call to ensure they're still available.

5.2: Attach any preliminary materials they might need to review beforehand, like an agenda or brief overview.

6. Meeting Day:

6.1: Arrive prepared and punctual.

6.2: Start with gratitude: Appreciate their time and the opportunity to further support their business.

6.3: Present your case, ensuring you listen as much as you speak. Understand their concerns, needs, and reservations.

6.4: Close with a clear call to action. Whether it's a follow-up meeting, a product demo, or sending a quote, ensure the next steps are clear.

7. Post-Meeting:

7.1: Send a thank you note, expressing gratitude for their time and recapping the main points discussed.

7.2: Address any concerns or additional questions they might have raised during the meeting.

7.3: Offer any additional information or resources they might need to make a decision.

Remember, the goal is not just to get a meeting but to further solidify the relationship you have with the client. Every interaction should be conducted with the utmost professionalism, respect, and understanding of their needs.

Sharon was a sales pro, and this information was relatively basic. However, it nudged Sharon to think about how she prepared for her call. She realized there was room for improvement.

She asked, *"Why would a furniture company exhibit at a tradeshow?"*

ChatGPT briefly touched on the following ten reasons:

- Brand Awareness and Exposure.
- Networking.
- New Product Launch.
- Market Trends and Insights.
- Sales Opportunities.
- Feedback.
- Strengthening Customer Relationships.
- Learning Opportunities.
- Market Expansion.
- Media Exposure.

This information was broad in scope, so Sharon altered her prompt and asked, *"A furniture company will be participating in an industry tradeshow. How does their booth help them attract leads?"*

The response included the following information:

Engaging Booth Design Includes:

- *Eye-catching: Bold colors, compelling graphics, and innovative designs can draw attendees' attention.*
- *Interactive Displays: Integrating technology like touchscreen displays or augmented reality to showcase furniture designs and features can captivate visitors.*

> • *Layout: The booth should be designed with clear pathways for visitors, making it easy for them to navigate and view the furniture pieces.*

The second bullet caught Sharon's eye, reminding her of a booth she sold another customer. It included a branded display built to hold a television monitor and to play videos.

Sharon decided to pitch this to Peter. Using ChatGPT, she created:

- An email asking for a meeting.
- A short presentation.
- An executive summary recapping the information in her presentation.

Peter agreed to meet. Once the meeting was scheduled, Sharon took one more step and asked ChatGPT: **What questions would a buyer ask a salesperson when considering a purchase for a tradeshow booth?**

ChatGPT provided 29 questions. Sharon felt comfortable answering all but two. She used ChatGPT as her virtual sales coach and developed solid answers.

The day of the meeting arrived, and Sharon was well-prepared to present to Peter. After some friendly chit-chat, she walked him through the presentation. It showcased her company's capabilities and how they could incorporate an interactive display for a video monitor in a booth design.

"I love that idea," Peter said. "We have loads of videos, and this would be a perfect solution to use them in our booth."

Then he asked, "What is the lead time for designing, producing, and delivering a booth like this?"

It was one of the questions provided by ChatGPT, and Sharon was ready to answer.

They talked for a few more minutes. Sharon handed Peter the executive summary she had created as the meeting wrapped up, detailing her company's capabilities, and linking them to benefits.

Peter studied the summary for a moment. He said, "I appreciate your effort in educating me about your company's tradeshow solutions, and I have been thinking about re-doing the booth. Let's put together a quote and see what you can do."

Sharon smiled. The call had gone great, and she was already considering using the same strategy to cross-sell to other customers.

A Quick Review

You can use ChatGPT in many ways to plan, prepare, and execute cross-selling strategies, including:

- Gathering insight on anything connected to selling something specific, like targeted industries, buyer pain points, product benefits, or reasons to change vendors.
- Analyzing competitive information.
- Writing product or service-specific emails to request a meeting.

- Creating presentations, case studies, executive summaries, or sell sheets to educate buyers and present benefits.
- Compiling lists of buyer questions or possible objections and preparing to win by developing scripted responses.
- Creating scenarios or examples as part of your meeting preparation.
- Providing feedback by using AI to analyze sales interactions and outcomes.

As you can see, there are many ways to use ChatGPT for cross-selling. Invest a little time and give it a try!

Chapter Fourteen

AI and Social Selling on LinkedIn

Many buyers use LinkedIn to find new suppliers. If you pop up during their search, they will look at your profile. Buyers also check out your profile when they are deciding whether or not they should meet with you, or after an initial meeting.

ChatGPT can help you with your LinkedIn strategy, including:

- Building your personal brand.
- Creating content.
- Building relationships.

Your Profile

Think about how you would like buyers in your world to see you. What values, characteristics, and behaviors do you want to come to mind instantly? And how can you project those values, characteristics, and behaviors in your LinkedIn social media profile?

Let's start by examining a vital concept: brand projection. Effective projection allows you to be 'heard,' even when you aren't involved in a face-to-face conversation with an audience. It communicates who you are and what you stand for, offering potential buyers the necessary knowledge to make empowered decisions.

Many factors define you as a sales professional. To narrow the field, answer three questions:

- What is your area of expertise in your market?
- How do you help your customers?
- How would you describe your business personality?

Let's look at an example.

Jerry was a sales pro who sold customer onboarding software to banks. He was an expert who understood efficient onboarding led to higher customer satisfaction and, ultimately, more bank profits. Jerry helped customers by educating them on a complex topic, including the value of efficient onboarding, the benefits of his company's software, and the implementation process. Jerry described his business personality as a 'helpful sales-focused accountant,' meaning he was an analytically minded sales pro who helped clients make a business case for purchasing his software by identifying the pain points of inefficient onboarding and assigning cost savings or increased profit dollars to areas for improvement.

Doing the exercise helped Jerry recognize his profile didn't reflect the personal brand he wanted to project. He decided to improve his profile with assistance from AI by taking the following steps:

- Ask ChatGPT to recommend keywords buyers would use when searching for the product or service.
- Update his professional summary.
- Develop a customized headline for his profile.
- Improve descriptions of his past experiences.

Jerry started with a prompt to discover keywords so he could include them in his descriptions, increasing the likelihood of being found by potential buyers. He asked: ***What keywords and search terms would a buyer who wanted to purchase onboarding software for a bank use to find a company or a salesperson using LinkedIn?***

ChatGPT returned over 20 possibilities. Jerry reviewed and narrowed the field to four primary options:

- Bank onboarding software.
- Financial institution onboarding system.
- Banking digital onboarding solution.
- Bank customer onboarding platform.

Jerry used the information he gathered from answering the three questions and compiled a short list of bulleted points to include in his 'About' Section. He input it into ChatGPT using this prompt: ***Write a compelling 'About' section for LinkedIn. Important keyword phrases are (1) bank onboarding software, (2) bank customer onboarding platform, and (3) banking digital onboarding solution. The 'About Me' section must project my expertise as a sales professional who sells customer onboarding software to*** *banks and financial institutions. Points to mention include:*

- *Ten years of experience selling onboarding software solutions.*
- *Expertise in helping clients choose the right solution and understanding the implementation process.*
- *The benefits of selecting the right onboarding software solution include the prevention of abandoned applications, better banking customer experience, and a more efficient process, which saves customer time and lowers expenses for banks.*
- *I understand the problems banks face that can be solved with the right customer onboarding software.*

Jerry queried ChatGPT, and the system responded with this copy:

Hello and welcome to my profile!

With over a decade immersed in the realm of bank onboarding software, I have dedicated my professional journey to empowering banks and financial institutions to seamlessly welcome their customers through the perfect digital onboarding experience. My passion lies at the intersection of technology and customer experience, where I've assisted countless banks in navigating the vast sea of bank customer onboarding platforms.

Having spent 10 enriching years selling onboarding software solutions, I pride myself not just on selling a product, but on

---

partnering with my clients to ensure they select the right solution tailored to their unique needs. More than just understanding the software, I have an innate knack for grasping the intricacies of the implementation process, ensuring a smooth transition and deployment every step of the way.

But why is choosing the right banking digital onboarding solution so crucial? The answer is manifold:

1. Prevent Abandoned Applications: In the digital age, first impressions matter. A seamless onboarding process ensures customers complete their applications without hiccups or hesitations.

2. Elevate Customer Experience: A fluid onboarding journey not only welcomes a customer but makes them feel valued and understood from day one.

3. Efficiency and Savings: Beyond the customer, the right platform streamlines processes, saves invaluable time, and significantly reduces operational expenses for banks.

At the core of my approach is a deep understanding of the challenges banks face daily. Whether it's compliance hurdles, shifting customer expectations, or operational inefficiencies, I recognize the problems and offer solutions powered by the latest in onboarding software innovations.

If you're passionate about enhancing your bank's customer onboarding journey and are in search of a dedicated, knowledgeable partner to guide you through, let's connect and craft the future together.

Jerry then asked, *"Based on this 'About Me' profile, suggest five possible LinkedIn headlines."*

ChatGPT responded with these suggestions:

> - *Digital Onboarding Maven | 10+ Years Elevating Banking Experiences with Top-tier Onboarding Software Solutions*
> - *Empowering Banks with Premier Onboarding Platforms | A Decade of Excellence in Banking Digital Solutions Sales*
> - *Banking Onboarding Specialist: Transforming Customer Journeys & Boosting Efficiency with Tailored Software Solutions*
> - *10 Years Perfecting Banks' First Impressions | Your Trusted Partner in Onboarding Software Selection & Implementation*
> - *Crafting Seamless Banking Experiences | Expert in Onboarding Software Solutions & Transformative Digital Strategies*

Jerry went with the third suggestion, did a little tweaking on the 'About' copy, and loaded everything into his profile.

Next, he worked on his 'Experience' section. Jerry currently had a single descriptive line explaining his sales role at his current employer that read, 'Account executive for customer onboarding software company selling to banking and financial institutions.'

Jerry wrote a prompt asking ChatGPT to write copy that effectively projected his personal brand. In the prompt, he outlined his key responsibilities and accomplishments.

The prompt said, *"Write a description for the LinkedIn experience section for my current position as an Account Executive at GTOnboard Software, selling customer onboarding software. I am responsible for a national sales territory, product consulting with financial institutions, and implementation after customers buy the software for GTOnboard Software. Accomplishments include consistent growth in sales revenues generated and one of the top three sales performers for seven years. Proud to say 92% of all customers sold are still partnering with GTOnboard Software and using the software I sold them."*

ChatGPT returned an answer, but the first response struck Jerry as a little long. He typed in *'Shorten the section,'* and the system instantly complied, offering this alternative.

Account Executive, GTOnboard Software

Championing national sales for GTOnboard Software's cutting-edge customer onboarding solutions, I'm proud to partner with financial institutions, offering tailored software that fits their unique needs.

Key Roles:

- *National Sales Oversight: Driving the adoption of our onboarding software across financial entities nationwide.*
- *Product Consulting: Engaging deeply with institutions to ensure our software aligns with their distinct challenges.*

- *Post-Sale Guidance: Seamlessly transitioning customers through the software implementation phase.*

Achievements:

- *Sales Growth: Consistently expanded our revenue streams, reflecting the trust our partners place in us.*
- *Recognition: Maintained a position among the top three sales performers for seven years.*
- *Long-term Partnerships: A whopping 92% of the institutions I've collaborated with remain loyal GTOnboard Software users.*

For those in the financial realm seeking a refined onboarding experience, I'm here to guide and ensure your success with GTOnboard Software.

Jerry thought the new section description worked well, and using ChatGPT to update was fast and easy. He quickly updated the other jobs listed in the Experience section, feeling he was on a roll!

Reviewing his profile also highlighted another area where Jerry recognized it could use improvement, so let's look at that.

Your Recommendation Section

Jerry had three testimonials from customers. He requested them when he first set up his LinkedIn page, so all were written several years earlier. Two of the testimonials were from current customers. Jerry started by asking for an updated testimonial and mentioning his subject matter expertise in banking. Since he had a strong relationship with the two customers and his request was simple, Jerry wrote a message without AI help and sent it off.

He also decided he would be more successful asking his customers for help if he first wrote recommendations for them, assisted by ChatGPT.

He decided to take this approach with Susan Bradley. She was the Chief Technology Officer at a regional bank with ten offices in four states. She was a fan of his technology because she believed it helped her bank improve the customers' experience.

Jerry wrote a prompt that said, *"Write a short LinkedIn recommendation for Susan Bradley, Chief Technology Officer at a regional bank. Susan is an expert in financial services technology, and I have sold Susan onboarding software. Susan is great to work with because she understands a better customer experience at all levels, including onboarding, leads to stronger banking relationships, more profitable customers, and less churn. Susan is also organized and a good communicator."*

ChatGPT's first attempt was well-written but still struck Jerry as long. So, he followed his first prompt with additional instructions: *Shorten the recommendation by 50%.*

ChatGPT complied with this:

> *I had the privilege of collaborating with Susan Bradley, CTO at her regional bank, during the rollout of our onboarding software. Susan's expertise in financial services technology is exceptional; she understands that a streamlined onboarding process leads to more profitable and long-lasting banking relationships.*
>
> *What sets Susan apart is her holistic view of customer experience. She is meticulous in optimizing every facet of the customer journey. Her organizational skills were evident in the punctual and budget-conscious completion of our project. In addition, Susan is a skilled communicator, simplifying complex technical terms for stakeholders at all levels.*
>
> *Simply put, Susan is a visionary leader in the financial services sector. She would be an invaluable asset to any organization. I highly recommend her.*

Jerry was happy with the shorter version and posted it for Susan to review. She thanked Jerry and accepted what he had written. He told her he appreciated her business and asked if she would mind writing a recommendation for him. She sent one the next day.

Since the strategy worked, Jerry selected another customer and took the same approach. This time he chose one of his newer customers, Marvin Smith, another Chief Technology Officer. Using ChatGPT, Jerry wrote a LinkedIn recommendation for Marvin.

Marvin was pleased to get the recommendation, but since Jerry didn't know Marvin as well as he knew Susan, he used ChatGPT to create a message asking Marvin for a recommendation. The prompt read: **Write a very short LinkedIn recommendation request for a happy client who is the Chief Technology Officer for a large bank with multiple locations. I have sold this client onboarding software and managed the implementation.**

ChatGPT responded:

Subject: Request for a LinkedIn Recommendation

Dear [Client's Name],

I hope this message finds you well. It was a pleasure working closely with you on the successful implementation of our onboarding software at your bank. I am reaching out to kindly ask if you could take a few moments to write a LinkedIn recommendation for me.

Your perspective as the CTO of a large, multi-location bank would provide valuable insight into our successful collaboration and the positive impact the software has had.

Thank you for considering my request. If you're short on time, I'd be happy to provide a draft for your convenience.

Best regards,

[Your Name]

Jerry tweaked the response, sent it to Marvin, and was happy when Marvin responded, saying he would be glad to write a recommendation.

After ChatGPT helped Jerry improve his profile and recommendations section, he looked for other ways to use AI in his social selling approach.

Keeping Your Personal Brand Visible

When a buyer is ready to buy, social selling helps you win under any of the following conditions:

- An unknown lead is looking for a new supplier. The buyer looks on LinkedIn to find options. They discover your profile, like what they see, and reach out.
- You are linked to the buyer but haven't sold them anything yet. However, your posts keep popping up in their LinkedIn feed. Every time the buyer sees a post, they are reminded of you. Top-of-mind awareness builds up over time. One day, they need your product or service and decide to reach out.
- You are linked to a customer that is a good candidate for growth. You follow the person and their company and like and comment on the buyer's posts. The buyer takes note of your interactions. They start liking your posts. Over time, you earn more mindshare than your competitors and start getting new opportunities.

ChatGPT is a helpful tool for content creation and relationship-building in social channels. To get started, look at your profile's 'Activity' section. It contains five categories: posts, comments, videos, images, and articles.

To keep it simple, we'll focus on posts, comments, and articles.

Posts get noticed because they are relevant and interest your audience. Possible topics include:

- Reposts of information shared by industry thought leaders that is relevant to your audience.
- Company news and announcements, which can be as easy as reposting messages from your company.
- Information about products and services.
- Answering frequently asked questions.
- "Day in the life" posts where you take people inside your facility to showcase processes, products, or services.

ChatGPT can assist you with writing posts and suggest hashtags to help people find information on a specific topic. LinkedIn lets you schedule posts, so creating and loading posts in batches will save you time.

Remember Jerry, our software sales pro? Here are examples of situations and prompts he could use to help craft social posts.

Situation	Prompt	Post
Repost Information: Jerry read an online article in *Strategy + Business* about customer loyalty	Write one line for a LinkedIn post advising banking customers to read an article in *Strategy +*	*Don't miss this eye-opening read in Strategy + Business on how customer loyalty directly impacts*

that was relevant to banking.	*Business* about customer loyalty and profitability.	*profitability in banking!*
News and Announcements: Jerry and his team consistently met all implementation deadlines for the fifth year.	My team has met all software implementation deadlines for our customers for five years straight. Write a two-line LinkedIn post to celebrate this achievement.	*Absolutely thrilled to announce that our team has consistently met all software implementation deadlines for our customers for 5 years running! A huge thank you to our dedicated team and amazing clients.*
Information About Products & Services: Jerry's company updated its onboarding software, improving cybersecurity.	My company announced we have completed a major update to improve cybersecurity features on our onboarding software. Write a three-line LinkedIn post to promote this. Tell people to	*Excited to share that we've rolled out a major update to enhance cybersecurity features on our onboarding software! Your data's safety is our top priority. For more details,*

	direct message me for more information in the third line.	*feel free to DM me anytime.*
FAQs: Potential customers often ask, "What kind of customer service is available?"	Write a LinkedIn post that starts with, "What kind of customer service is available?" Tell people support is available 24/7, and includes live chat and phone support. Include, "Reach out if for details."	*"What kind of customer service is available?" A question we often hear and are proud to answer: Our support team is available 24/7, offering both live chat and phone support to assist you. Reach out for details!*
Day in the Life: The company holds a meeting at headquarters to share research and development plans for the upcoming year. Jerry takes a picture before the session starts and decides to post it.	Write a one-line LinkedIn post telling my community I am excited to meet with the R&D team and learn about plans for improving our onboarding software.	*Thrilled to meet with the R&D team today and dive into the upcoming enhancements for our onboarding software!*

Along with using ChatGPT to make it easier for Jerry to post more frequently, he wants to use AI to add thoughtful comments to posts written by his customers.

Marvin, the Chief Technology Officer who gave Jerry a recommendation, posted: ***I am pleased to announce that we have achieved a year of record growth in customer acquisition and technological advancements. I sincerely thank our dedicated team and loyal customers for contributing to this milestone.***

Jerry pasted Marvin's post into ChatGPT. He told the system that the copy was a LinkedIn post and added these instructions: ***Write a one-line comment I can post on LinkedIn acknowledging the achievement.***

ChatGPT responded with this post: *Congratulations to the entire team for this remarkable achievement; your dedication and hard work have truly paid off.*

As you read that, you might wonder, "What's so special about that?"

As is often the case with answers generated by Natural Language Processing (NLP), you may not feel it produced anything surprising or unknown. But it always provides a starting point, which keeps you moving forward, accomplishing tasks, and, ultimately, selling more.

Another way to keep your brand visible is by posting longer-form articles as content.

Social media posts quickly become buried in feeds. LinkedIn articles have a longer shelf life. You can feature them on your profile, and topics are searchable, providing more potential for engagement. Plus, they position you as a credible expert and offer value to your audience, making them more likely to engage.

Examples include:

- Articles to promote expertise and thought leadership.
- Industry insights.
- Case studies.
- Product or service descriptions.
- Long-form answers to cover complex FAQs.

The following are tips on writing prompts for each category:

Content	Tips for Your Prompt
Article	First, write a "tell me about" prompt that collects information on your topic. Then combine the information with your expertise to write a second prompt covering the following points: • Topic. • Target audience. • Key points to cover. • Article length (300 to 1,000 words, depending on the subject).
Industry Insights	When you spot information worth sharing, note essential points and

	relevant data. Your prompt should include: • The topic. • Target audience. • Key facts and relevant data. • Your interpretation and observations. • Any recommended actions. • Article length (300 to 500 words) Be sure to cite where you got your information, either in a mention or by linking to the source.
Case Studies	In Chapter 9, we discussed creating case studies for sales calls. This content category is very effective for social selling because it builds credibility and demonstrates value. Your prompt should include: • Title. • A summary of the situation and outcome. • Relevant background information. • The client's challenge and decision-making process. • Your solution: what it was and why it was selected.

	• The result, including a testimonial if the client is willing to provide one. • Case study length (300 to 750 words).
Product or Service Descriptions	Showcasing a product or service educates your audience and increases your visibility. Your prompt should include: • Title. • Information about the product or service. • Your interpretation or observations. • Why the client should act. • The action you want clients to take. • Length (300 to 750 words).
Answers to Complex FAQs	If you need help getting started on this, ask ChatGPT to generate a list of FAQs for the product or service you sell. Pick one and write a prompt covering the following: • What is the question, and why do customers often ask it? • The answer. • Length (300 to 500 words).

The following are a few other general tips to consider when creating social selling content:

- If you don't like a title recommendation, ask ChatGPT to give you five to ten options.
- Remember, you can specify the 'tone;' of the writing. For an article, the tone could be 'upbeat and professional.' For a case study, it could be 'direct, factual, and concise.' The possibilities are endless!
- If you don't like what you get the first time, you have three options for improvement. Hit the 'Regenerate' button and get a different version, edit your original prompt, or write instructions to tweak the results, like a follow-up prompt that says, "***Rewrite with a different opening paragraph and reduce the length of the article by a third.***"
- Include a call-to-action appropriate for the content.
- If you do a lot of rewriting and want to check your revision for grammar and spelling, you can drop the content back into ChatGPT with a prompt asking for a review.

Last Thoughts

We started by discussing improving your profile and adding recommendations to showcase your personal brand. Once you show to advantage, you want to maintain a visible presence and strengthen relationships. ChatGPT can help you create engaging posts and longer-form content. Commenting on your community's posts helps build and strengthen relationships, and AI can also help there if needed.

These tactics help you be 'heard,' even when you aren't involved in face-to-face conversations and give potential buyers the knowledge they need to make empowered decisions. By leveraging these strategies, you amplify your voice as a sales professional and establish yourself as a thought leader in your industry.

Chapter Fifteen

More on Writing Prompts

As a sales pro, you already know how to ask questions and request information, providing a natural understanding of how to write ChatGPT prompts. This chapter will look at ways to improve output by considering a range of important factors.

Know Your Goal

In sales, goals occur on three levels. Top-level goals reflect what you are striving to accomplish in terms of your overall sales, like opening three accounts in the next quarter. Second-level goals focus on specific accounts, like converting an active prospect into a first-time customer. Third-level goals are about the steps required to make second, and, ultimately, first-level goals happen. For example, to sell a new account, the first step is scheduling an initial discovery meeting with a contact. Prompts work best when written with a clear goal, so look for a way to include purpose in your instructions.

Be Specific

Broad-based prompts return broad-based answers. Sometimes, you seek mind-expanding thinking; other times, you want usable information as quickly as possible. When you want fast, helpful information, be specific. Include relevant details about who, what, why, where, and how.

Describe Your Audience

If you want a buyer to pay attention to information, make it relevant. When you use ChatGPT to create relevant information, your prompt should include details about the audience and their challenges. For example, you could say, "The audience is the Vice President of Sourcing at a food manufacturer." Or you could get even more granular and include further details, like, "The audience is the Vice President of Sourcing at a food manufacturer. They are new to the position but will be familiar with my company because we are an industry leader. Currently, they are not seeing growth in their sales, which could mean they are facing supply chain challenges." When it comes to being specific, use your sales intelligence to include details that motivate your audience to pay attention, read your words and say, "This applies to me!"

Provide Context

Context is your ally if you are aiming for a response that hits the mark. Just as you'd tailor a sales pitch to resonate with a specific buyer by thinking about that buyer's circumstances, prompts get better results when you include precise details that apply to the situation. For example, if you are writing an email to introduce a long-time customer to a new product, you would communicate differently than if you are writing an email to a cold lead. Taking a minute to set the stage provides a more targeted answer and often saves time by reducing the need for follow-up prompts.

You Can Use Open-Ended or Close-Ended Questions in a Prompt

Open-ended questions work best in scenarios that call for in-depth exploration, critical thinking, and creative thinking, such as researching a topic. In contrast, close-ended questions are the go-to choice for quick, straightforward answers or quantitative data.

When asking open-ended questions, you may want to include a "temperature setting" mentioned in an earlier chapter in your prompt. Here is how ChatGPT explains temperature settings:

The "temperature" is a hyperparameter that controls the randomness of the model's output. It ranges from 0 to 1:

A lower temperature value (e.g., 0.2) will make the model's output more focused and deterministic, sticking closely to the most likely completion. This is useful when you want very consistent and less random responses.

A higher temperature value (e.g., 0.8 or 1) introduces more randomness, making the model's output more diverse and

Narrow the Field

Limiting a prompt to one question or topic leads to better-focused answers, even when it is a broad question or a big issue. Knowing your goal keeps you focused. Sticking with short, direct sentences ensures you stay on point and get usable answers.

Specify the Format

If you want information for a specific type of communication, like an email, social post, or article, specify the format and include a word count.

Specify Parameters

If you want ChatGPT to generate multiple options, define the parameters. Include phrases like, "Give me three options."

Specify the Tone or Style

Let's say you use AI to write an introductory email to a new lead. Do you want the tone to be professional, informative, conversational, friendly, or authoritative? Or maybe the style you want to achieve is best described by combining adjectives like helpful, professional, and informative.

When you write a prompt to include your preference about the desired tone, ChatGPT will accommodate. Or you can go one step further and ask ChatGPT to adopt a persona and write in that style. The persona could represent an archetype or an actual person.

Let's look at how personas change outcomes by looking at a prompt tied to introducing a new product called the Widgeto 5000.

Adding a Persona to the Prompt	Response
Write one line to introduce a new product called the Widgeto 5000 in the style of a seasoned sales manager.	*Introducing the Widgeto 5000—your one-stop solution for efficiency, reliability, and performance; this is the game-changer you've been waiting for!*
Write one line to introduce the Widgeto 5000 in the style of sales legend Zig Ziglar.	*Introducing the Widgeto 5000—your golden ticket to a life of ease, efficiency, and excellence!*
Write one line to introduce the Widgeto 5000 in the style of advertising legend David Ogilvy.	*Introducing the Widgeto 5000: The revolutionary device that redefines your everyday, making the impossible, possible.*
Write one line to introduce the Widgeto 5000 in the style of a TikTok influencer.	*Say hello to the Widgeto 5000, y'all—this is the game-changer you didn't know you needed!*

While including tone or style instructions adds an extra step to a prompt, this strategic move can also make sales communications more impactful.

Ask ChatGPT to Generate Questions

Sometimes, you have a vague idea of what you want to accomplish but need help turning your initial concept into actionable communication. One way to move forward is by asking ChatGPT to generate questions. Sift through the questions and use whatever is appropriate to construct a better prompt.

Let's look at an example using this prompt: ***What questions would buyers ask themselves if they are considering switching vendors?***

ChatGPT responded:

> *When buyers are considering switching vendors, they may ask themselves a variety of questions to evaluate the decision. Here are some common questions they might ponder:*
>
> *Cost and Value*
>
> > *1. Will the new vendor offer better pricing?*
> > *2. Is the value proposition stronger with the new vendor?*
> > *3. Are there hidden costs associated with switching?*
>
> *Quality and Reliability*
>
> > *1. Does the new vendor offer better quality products or services?*

2. What is the track record of the new vendor in terms of reliability?
3. Are there any quality assurance certifications or guarantees?

Compatibility and Integration

1. How easily can the new vendor's products or services be integrated into our existing systems?
2. Is the new vendor compatible with our company culture and values?

Customer Service and Support

1. Does the new vendor offer better customer service?
2. What are the support options and are they available 24/7?

Contractual Obligations

1. Are there any penalties or costs for terminating the contract with the current vendor?
2. What are the terms and conditions of the new vendor's contract?

Scalability and Future Growth

1. Can the new vendor accommodate our future growth plans?
2. Is the new vendor more innovative and adaptable to market changes?

Risk Assessment

1. What are the risks involved in switching vendors?

> *2. How will the switch affect our operations in the short-term and long-term?*
>
> *Reviews and Recommendations*
>
> > *1. What do other customers say about the new vendor?*
> > *2. Are there any industry awards or recognitions that the new vendor has received?*
>
> *Logistics and Delivery*
>
> > *1. Does the new vendor offer better delivery times or options?*
> > *2. How does the new vendor handle returns or defective products?*
>
> *These questions can help buyers make a more informed decision about whether or not to switch vendors.*

Starting with a list of questions can be invaluable for reverse-engineering prompts. It also helps you step into the buyer's shoes and address their concerns, increasing the relevancy of your communications.

Have a Dialogue

Starting with an initial prompt and then engaging in further dialogue with ChatGPT allows for a more nuanced and tailored conversation. The initial prompt provides a general direction for the discussion. Subsequent interactions enable you to clarify, expand upon, or redirect the chat based on the responses. Both you and ChatGPT adapt in a dynamic environment where each iteration takes you closer to generating content aligned with your ultimate objectives.

Last Thoughts on Powerful Prompts

Prompt writing is a skill you as a sales pro can quickly master because questioning and gathering information is already part of what you do daily.

The best way to get the hang of writing prompts is by using the system. Experiment and learn. Before long, you'll grasp the nuances that make you a prompt-producing dynamo, who uses ChatGPT and other AI systems to speed up sales cycles, connect more deeply with prospects, and close deals more efficiently.

Chapter Sixteen

Go Time!

Sales is a rewarding profession, financially and personally. You make a difference daily by helping your clients meet their needs, eliminate problems, and improve situations. By helping your company meet its revenue goals, you fund paychecks for yourself and your coworkers.

I am proud to be a sales professional, and I wrote this book because I believe that best-in-class sales pros never stop learning and are always looking for new ways to apply knowledge, improve outcomes, and sell more.

AI is a game changer for the business world, just like the Internet was. If you're reading this book, you recognize that—which is good for you. And there is more good news for us early adopters. Most salespeople haven't considered how they can use AI, so jumping in early gives YOU a competitive advantage.

Two other areas I encourage you to investigate are ChatGPT plugins and alternative systems. Plugins are third-party applications that give ChatGPT additional functionality, like handling specialized tasks.

We've implemented initial support for plugins in ChatGPT. Plugins are tools designed specifically for language models with safety as a core principle and help ChatGPT access up-to-date information, run computations, or use third-party services. Plugins can help you write better prompts, run calculations, summarize PDFs and online articles, and more. Many plugins are free.

Google developed an alternative to ChatGPT called "Bard." Microsoft partnered with ChatGPT to integrate AI into its search engine, Bing. IBM has Watson to provide generative AI capabilities to enterprise-level accounts. These are three prominent names, but many innovative companies are rushing to develop solutions.

Congratulations to you. Generative AI will transform sales as a profession. Right now, you are way ahead of the rest of the pack. Go and apply what you learned to keep your lead.

Good selling and best wishes for BIG success!